marriage to MURDER

marriage to MURDER

my story...
SHEILA GARVIE

With an Introduction and Postscript by
Laurence Dowdall

CHAMBERS

The publishers would like to thank the following for
kind permission to reproduce copyright photographs.
(The pages of the section of photographs in the centre
of the book have here been numbered 1 – 16 for
convenience.)
  Scottish Daily Record and Sunday Mail Ltd for
pages 4, 9 (above), 10, 11, 12, 13 and 14
  Glasgow Herald and Evening Times for pages 8, 9
(below) and 15 (above)
  The photographs on pages 5, 6 and 7 are from the
picture library of the Scottish Daily Record and
Sunday Mail Ltd

First published 1980 by W & R Chambers Ltd,
Edinburgh

Set by
Hewer Text Composition Services, Edinburgh
and printed in Great Britain
by Clark Constable Ltd, Edinburgh

ISBN 0 550 20356 7

This book is dedicated to Lady Martha Bruce,
present Governor of Cornton Vale Prison, and all who, like
her, are devoted to prison reform in the belief that
'the loss of freedom is punishment enough'.
It is also dedicated to all those people amongst staff and fellow
prisoners who helped and supported me during
ten long years of imprisonment.

*The author and publishers wish to express their sincere
appreciation of the collaboration of Alison Goodall in the
preparation of this book.*

Introduction
by Laurence Dowdall

About the end of May 1968 I was idly turning over the pages of my newspaper when I read of the disappearance of a wealthy farmer from Fordoun in Kincardineshire. I was interested principally because I knew the area well, having worked often in Aberdeen and Stonehaven and having travelled fairly extensively in the Mearns (as the county, now Kincardine District, has always been more commonly called).

The circumstances of the disappearance—according to the reports—were strange. The farmer, who piloted his own aeroplane, had left the plane in the hangar at Fordoun airstrip, while the car he had been using had been found adjacent to the hangar with the door locked and the choke out.

My interest, of course, was a passing one and as the days went on the news petered out.

But my attention was attracted again when I happened to read, in the *Police Gazette* of 14 June 1968, a reference to this missing farmer with the following remarkable description: 'Spends freely. Is a heavy spirit drinker and often consumes tranquillisers and Pro-Plus tablets when drinking. Is fond of female company but has strong homosexual tendencies and is often in company of young men. . . . Deals in pornographic material and is an active member of nudist camps. . . . May have gone abroad.'

Not knowing anything more about him, I did not wonder that he should have gone abroad, and I promptly forgot all about it. These things do happen.

On 20 August 1968, however, my newspaper bore banner headlines in black type: MURDER BY SHOOTING—

followed by an announcement in type not quite so large but equally eyecatching: 'The widow of wealthy farmer Maxwell Garvie was yesterday named as one of three people charged with his murder.' The dramatic report went on to narrate that the other two on a similar charge of murder by shooting were Brian Tevendale, of Aberdeen, and Alan Peters, of Fort Augustus. Apparently the names had been read out to the eager pressmen by the Procurator Fiscal at Stonehaven. The report narrated that until that day Stonehaven Sheriff Court had not heard a murder charge read out in more than seventy years. A spokesman for the Scottish and North-Eastern Counties Constabulary announced that a body found in a water-filled drainage pit had been positively identified as that of Garvie, who had vanished on Thursday 14 May 1968.

My professional interest was thus awakened, although I did not know that I would figure in the defence of one of the three accused. That day, however, I received a telephone call from a well-known Aberdeen solicitor which electrified me. Would I come to Aberdeen to see him with a view to taking over the defence of Mrs Sheila Garvie?

The following morning I flew to Aberdeen and called on the solicitor at his office. He told me he had seen Mrs Garvie at Police Headquarters at Bucksburn following her arrest and that one of his colleagues had appeared with her at Stonehaven Sheriff Court. All three accused were committed for further examination and remanded to Craiginches Prison. They had to appear for full committal on 26 August 1968. He had suggested to Mrs Garvie that I should take over the defence and she had agreed to see me. He himself had made no enquiries into the matter with which she was charged.

I left his office and went to Craiginches Prison for the first of my many interviews with Sheila Garvie. She was brought into the Interviewing Room by a female prison officer and we were left alone. She was dressed in a prison frock and, despite her deadly pallor and lack of make-up, she was a very attractive woman. I rose to meet her, told her my name and said 'Your solicitor has told me that you would like me to act for you.'

2

Quietly, she thanked me. She was obviously very apprehensive and nervous—a timid, tearful, bewildered woman. At this stage she mistrusted everyone. The interview was difficult, filled with awkward pauses, but after half an hour I began to make some progress. Gradually the barrier came down. She relaxed and it became clear to me that the one thing she needed above all was someone to talk to. I told her there was no need to tell me anything about the story there and then, but I enquired about the circumstances of her arrest and asked her if she had made a statement to the police. She said that she had. I told her that I would come back after I had made some enquiries and that I would see her in Stonehaven Sheriff Court on 26 August when she would appear for full committal.

On the morning of 26 August I appeared with her in chambers at the Sheriff Court before Sheriff J Aikman Smith. Mrs Garvie had been brought to the building from a police car, completely covered by a blanket. I intimated that she did not intend to make any declaration. She and the two others, who were represented by local solicitors, were committed until liberation in due course of law.

Later that day I again saw Mrs Garvie at Craiginches Prison. At that meeting I asked her if she knew Tevendale and Peters: she told me that Tevendale she knew but Peters she had never seen prior to the shooting incident.

I was most anxious not to discuss the matter with her until I was fully in the picture with regard to the evidence of the Crown. Our conversation was therefore restricted to describing the procedure which would take place—culminating in the eventual trial in the High Court. I could sense that by this time she trusted me and would be prepared to talk. I told her at that meeting that when next I saw her I would be in a position to advise her what she was facing in the way of evidence.

I then wrote to the Crown Office to enquire if I could have a preliminary list of prosecution witnesses, and as usual they provided it. Having written to the Chief Constable of the North-Eastern Counties Constabulary and received permission to interview the police witnesses, I called by appointment at Police Headquarters at Bucksburn. As usual, the police were most helpful. I was told that Max Garvie's body might never have been found and a murder investigation might not have got under way but for the action of Mrs Garvie's mother, Mrs Edith Watson. I learned that on 16 August, some twelve weeks after Max Garvie's disappearance, Mrs Watson had arrived at the home of his farm grieve (foreman), in a state of hysteria, with a garbled story to the effect that he would never see Maxie again. He promptly took her to the police.

After a doctor had been called and a sedative given to her, the distraught Mrs Watson poured out her story. This clearly implicated her daughter Sheila and Sheila's lover, Brian Tevendale, in the disappearance of Maxwell Garvie. Up till then, for the sake of her daughter, Mrs Watson had concealed her knowledge but eventually the weight on her conscience proved too much and now the secret was out. As a consequence Mrs Garvie, Tevendale and Alan Peters, a friend of Tevendale, were arrested.

The police gave me copies of the astonishing statements made under caution by the three accused. They were diametrically opposed and completely irreconcilable.

I was aware from the evidence I had gathered that there was an affair of some sexual magnitude between Sheila Garvie and Brian Tevendale and that Tevendale's sister, Mrs Trudy Birse, was similarly accommodating Maxwell Garvie. I was puzzled because Sheila Garvie did not seem to be the type of woman to become involved in a sexual misadventure of this kind.

Armed with all my information I then paid a visit to Craiginches Prison to interview Mrs Garvie again. I wanted, of course, to know how this sordid state of affairs had developed. I did not reveal to her at the beginning that I had a copy of the statements made by the three accused to the police.

The sexual theme was an awkward subject to broach with this attractive young woman whom I hardly knew, but it had to be done. I said 'I know how distasteful this must be for you, but it is absolutely vital to your defence that you are

4

completely frank with me. I have to know every detail about the relationship between you and Tevendale on the one hand and Tevendale's sister and your deceased husband on the other. There is no need for you to be shy or embarrassed. I have been a practising criminal lawyer for many years and there is nothing you can tell me that I have not heard before.' (In that, however, I was mistaken!)

There was a pause, and hesitantly she began her story. 'It is all so horrible I don't know where to begin. We were very happy once but Max changed so much. It was like a nightmare.' Bit by bit she unfolded an amazing tale of intrigue, sexual licence and deviation. I have the faded precognition I took at Craiginches Prison before me now as I write.

Mrs Garvie's story was a long one, and it was some time before we arrived at the evening of 14 May 1968. But her version of the events of that night was the same in every detail as the one she had told the police. That statement, she assured me, had been made of her own volition. I then produced the copy I had of it and read it over to her. When I had finished reading, she began to sob. She wept bitterly as she explained 'I was on my knees clutching the handle of the girls' bedroom as they dragged the body down the stairs!'

It was a horrendous picture, but if her story was true she was not guilty of murder.

The interview had been a lengthy one and I could see that Mrs Garvie was completely exhausted. I told her I would make further enquiries, and left her.

The Garvie trial monopolised the attention of the entire Scottish press and many of the national dailies for the best part of a fortnight. It was truly sensational, and will undoubtedly be among the best-remembered of recent British murder trials. It was a case, moreover, which we might well have won. Very little stood between Sheila Garvie and acquittal.

The story Sheila Garvie told me that day in Craiginches Prison is the same one that she tells today, twelve years later. Throughout the three days during which she gave evidence in court she steadfastly refused, under relentless cross-examination, to depart from the accounts she had given the police. She never has departed from them since.

Sheila Garvie has only recently been released from prison after losing ten years of her life. Now, when the processes of law have run their course, I think Sheila Garvie's story deserves a second hearing.

1

Until the morning of Tuesday 19 November 1968, when I entered the dock of Aberdeen High Court, I had never imagined that a murder trial could stir the blood of so many ordinary people or infuse them with such a fever of curiosity.

I could see the excited crowds gathered in the streets around the courthouse as I arrived. Hundreds of people had queued for hours on that cold, damp winter's day in the hope of getting a seat on the public benches. The hostile, disapproving eyes of the women and the gaping, eager faces of the men etched their reflections on my memory as they pushed and jostled for better positions to see this disreputable woman who had brought shame and disgrace to her family and had defamed the very soil of the Mearns.

My legs shook and my body trembled with nerves as I climbed the steps into the dock of the grim, high-ceilinged courtroom. I had had no conception that this trial was to cause such a sensation.

They had all come to see me. I was on trial for the murder of my husband, Maxwell Robert Garvie, whose body had been found in an underground tunnel near the little village of St Cyrus in Kincardineshire. One of my co-accused, Brian Tevendale—the young man with whom I had fallen in love—sat on my left in the dock. The other, Alan Peters—a young friend of Brian's I hardly knew—sat on my right. The stage was set, the drama about to unfold.

How had this nightmare come about? All around me there was only blackness and hostile stares. I couldn't believe that this was actually happening.

I had had a strict upbringing in a decent, God-fearing

family, in which the very mention of the word 'sex' was taboo. My childhood had been a happy one, and three years of my young life had been spent in the beautiful surroundings of the Royal Estate at Balmoral, where my father had been the estate mason. A little later I had been assistant to the Balmoral Castle housekeeper and was very well thought of. And until I married Max Garvie I was a Sunday School teacher. Honesty, truth and decency had been bred into me in a home where there was no room for displays of swank and swagger. But I had possessed the capacity both to love passionately and to hate with an unforgiving heart. It was this which diverted me from the 'straight and narrow' path. There had been no big neon signs flashing—Halt! Only fools rush in here! There were no alarm bells clanging as I hastened on my way to self-destruction. Before I knew it, I had been catapulted into the jaws of justice, to be swallowed up remorse-lessly by the tide of public opinion.

From the moment I stepped into the dock until sentence was pronounced ten days later, I hardly reflected on what the outcome of my trial would be. It was as if I was a one-woman audience watching a macabre pantomime. I never thought about what would happen when the curtain came down.

I scanned the scene before my eyes that morning. There they sat, the legal profession; symbols of law, honour and virtue, representatives of society poised to steady the scales of justice and demand fair play for all. Draped in their gowns they perched on chairs and benches or huddled in groups round tables, rustling papers and flipping through the pages of musty-looking law books which sprawled and littered the table-tops in front of them. Now and again one of them would turn to take a covert look at me.

They talked in hushed voices amongst themselves, their sombre wigs tilted at varying angles as they reached to scratch their heads or adjust their spectacles.

Suddenly I jumped a little as the court vibrated to the harsh blare of trumpets and double doors above the platform opened wide. A man in a scarlet and white gown made a swift but dignified entrance and the black-robed intelligentsia

8

beneath him almost knocked over their chairs in their haste to spring to their feet and bow.

With a faint heart I studied this man—the judge, Lord Thomson—as he took his seat, seemingly unaware of the gymnastics in his honour. He looked very solemn beneath his mop of false curls. His mouth seemed to me tight and humourless and his eyes cold and unemotional. I could feel the tension, the fever, the excitement in the court begin to build up. Fear clutched at my throat. I gripped my knees in an effort to stop them trembling. In a split second I realised that my whole life lay in the mind, heart and judgment of this court and a tremulous shudder passed through me. My mouth was parched and dry with panic—the kind of fear that not even the powerful tranquillisers given to me by the policewoman could control. What has been called one of the most sensational criminal trials in Scotland's history was about to begin—and I was in the dock!

The jurors were sworn in and took their seats nervously. They were all ordinary-looking people, the kind of folk you see—or rather, overlook—in the course of a busy day's shopping in town. They were a motley assortment: a mixture of tweeds, Fair Isle sweaters, dark navy 'Sunday' suits and stiff white collars, handbags, headsquares and crisp, starched handkerchiefs. I counted. There were nine men and six women.

One juror, a red-faced, weatherbeaten man, looked more anxious than the rest and I wondered if he had already begun to worry about his pigs. Had the sow farrowed yet and would the litter fetch a good market price?

None of these people had asked to come here, and I wondered if each of them was endowed with enough intellect, reason and wisdom to judge guilt or innocence. I didn't envy them their task. They looked uncomfortable and would have much preferred, no doubt, to have been at home feeding their stock, stirring their pots or gossiping with the neighbours.

Suddenly my thoughts about the people in court were sharply interrupted by a loud call from the macer, summoning the first important witness for the prosecution. 'Mrs Edith Watson. . . !'

It was my mother.

This was the first time I had seen her since the day, three months earlier, when she had relinquished all claims to my love.

I was not grieved so much by the fact that it was she who was responsible for my arrest, for thirty-three hours of non-stop questioning by detectives and for the murder charge against me. What really broke my heart was the sure and certain knowledge that she had betrayed my trust and confidence. And she was the only person on earth I would have trusted completely. That was why I had told her two days after the crime had been committed that Max had not 'vanished' but was in fact dead.

She had kept that dreadful secret for three months. Had she continued to keep it, as I was certain she would, and had she not gone to the police that Friday, it is possible that to this day the disappearance of the 'flying farmer'—as people called him—would still be an unsolved mystery, a dusty, forgotten file on a shelf.

We had enjoyed a very special relationship, my mother and I: one that had become enriched as the years went by and made other friendships pale in comparison. We had laughed together, cried together and shared family joys and sorrows. I could talk to her, not only as a daughter but also as a close and understanding friend who was always there to listen, advise and comfort. The only problems I could never fully share with her were sexual ones. She had always been deaf and blind to anything connected with the subject.

Her weary shoulders drooped now as she climbed slowly into the witness box and swore to tell the truth. A cold, impersonal voice asked her 'Do you recognise the accused?'

Our eyes met.

From that moment of recognition, all the feelings of contempt I had harboured for my mother during my three-month remand in Craiginches Prison were washed away. A great wave of love and compassion welled up inside me—as did tears, which poured uncontrollably down my face. I struggled to remain composed, but my mother was unable to control her grief and I watched in agonised despair as she was carried from the court in a state of collapse, that one question still unanswered. I wanted to run and throw my arms around her. That harrowing scene will remain with me for the rest of my life.

But at least my eyes had been opened to my mother's genuine distress. For all those months in prison I had been so blinded by emotion that I had not understood that my mother had simply done what she thought was best for me. She had gone to the police because her natural instincts as a mother were to protect her young. She was looking from the outside into the web of wrongdoing in which I was trapped— a web so tight and strong that I couldn't see the gathering clouds of self-destruction which were plain to her. Moreover, she had not known the whole truth.

My mother was ill even at the beginning of my trial. She died in May 1969, six months after I had been convicted of murder. She was buried quietly in Stonehaven and I was not allowed to leave my cell in Gateside Prison, Greenock, to attend her funeral.

The day she was buried a prison officer gave me a letter from her. It read:

'My Dearest Sheila,

'If you ever receive this I will be with my Mum and Dad. Don't ever grieve for me except that if you are still in Gateside I will not be with the bairns and that thought is terrible to me, however, you cannot bargain with God, if I could, I would gladly give up my life to be able to let you free. Don't ever give up, keep your head high, you were never bad, never, so always remember that. If I can I will be looking after you from somewhere so think of me standing beside you always. It was, if we had known, the saddest part of your life when you married into the Garvies, no wonder I cried all the time you were being married. You have always been greatly loved by me and the love I have for you has never changed, although perhaps at one time you thought so. I cannot write more, my heart is too full at having to leave you and the bairns so please let God bless you and may you be happy yet as I think you will. All my love forever until we meet again,

'Your most loving

'Mother.

'Sheila,

'I think I was only given about this time by the doctors in Aberdeen so all the recent happenings had actually nothing to do with my illness.'

I read the letter, knowing that as I read it my mother's funeral was taking place far away in Stonehaven. I couldn't hold back the tears, and I was taken to the medical room, given two aspirin and escorted back to my cell. I collapsed on the little narrow bed and broke my heart.

2

Tragedy struck at a very early age. My first memory is of sitting in my pram, at the age of about two, near a white rose bush on a hot summer's day. Along came a huge, fat bumble bee and stung me on the face. I howled with pain and the tears flowed, but my mother was there to remove the bee-sting and soothe and comfort her baby daughter.

We lived in Brickfield, Stonehaven. It was a tiny housing estate at that time and I don't imagine I would recognise any of it now. My father was a typical Scots 'head of the family', strict and uncompromising. The thing he hated most was noise in the house. If my sister and I started shouting, giggling or generally clattering around as youngsters do, a sharp word from Father soon put a stop to it. He also loathed the radio. If I wanted to listen to 'that noisy thing' I had to turn it down very low and put my ear right up against it.

If I needed comfort or someone to talk to it was always Mother I clung to. Father was distant, and although he did do 'fatherly' things like making us toys there was little show of affection from him. Mind you, he never hit either my sister or myself. He never needed to, as the sharp tone of his voice was enough to stop any childish nonsense or what he considered bad behaviour.

I think my mother felt sorry for us being targets for Father's strictness and often tried to cover up things we had done that she knew would get us into trouble with the head of the family. But on one particular day, nothing could save us from his wrath. My sister took me for a long walk—in my slippers—and dusk had already fallen by the time the pair of us got back to the house. Both my parents had been walking

13

the nearby streets and paths for hours, looking for us, and Father gave us a terrible row when we finally got back.

His temper, however, sometimes exploded in other directions. One day when I was about five a neighbourhood lad—a big red-haired fellow much older than us—got hold of my skipping rope, tied it around my neck and pulled. Father just happened to be looking out of the window at the time, saw what had happened—and saw red. He seized the lad's father and in a furious rage shook him like a dog by the collar!

I had to attend Sunday School from an early age and under no circumstances was even a suggestion of bad language ever allowed in the house.

At mealtimes, we stayed quiet and were taught the very best of table manners. One day during wartime a guest to our house brought along a real treasure of a gift for us all—a box of cakes, not the easiest of delicacies to obtain during those days. The cakes were placed carefully on the table, and as we sat down to tea I put out my hand to grab one and received—from Father—a sharp, well-placed kick on the shin under the table. That was my punishment for being too greedy and forgetting my manners.

We were well-brought-up children, taught to stay in line and behave well at all times, but I would have welcomed a little more love and warmth from my own father.

At school—I went to Dunnottar Primary—I was a bit of a tomboy, usually preferring to play cowboys and Indians with older boy cousins than at dolls and 'houses' with other little girls. The thing I really hated more than anything else was sewing, because I was left-handed and got everything round the wrong way! I moved on to start classes at the Mackie Academy only a matter of weeks before the family left Stonehaven to set up a new home on the Royal Deeside Estate at Balmoral.

My father had turned down the job at first because the pay was too low. Even a good job like estate mason only merited about £3.50 a week, which wasn't much even in those days at the end of the war. But it was a great honour to be asked to work for the Royal Family on their beautiful Highland estate, and finally he was persuaded to take on the

14

job. Just as I was coming up for twelve the Watsons moved, lock, stock and barrel, to set up their new home in the 'Artists' Rooms', only one hundred yards from the back entrance to Balmoral Castle.

Like any other child, I was sorry to leave Brickfield and the friends I had made at school and although everyone kept telling us how wonderful it was going to be living on the royal estate, the idea didn't excite me at all.

Gradually, however, I warmed to the beauty of the place. The summers always seemed to be long and hot and the tall, majestic evergreen trees were everywhere, their long, sweeping branches offering shade on the hottest days. The Castle itself was surrounded by luscious lawns, rose gardens and flowering shrubbery and I can still remember the heavy fragrance of the flowers that burst into bloom every year just before the Royal Family arrived for their annual holiday.

The 'Artists' Rooms' got their name in Queen Victoria's reign when she invited her favourite painters to capture the beauty of the estate and its surroundings. For a long time I could never understand why door and wall hooks in our house were so high and beyond my reach unless I stood on a chair. Then one day someone explained to me that they'd been put there at the request of the artist Landseer—who was a very tall man!

Looking at the house from the front, there were two archways and two turrets. Our section was on the left and our turret was the kitchen. You walked inside to a spacious, stone-floored hallway, off which was the laundry room. Up the stone stairway was a landing, a living room and three bedrooms, all large rooms with a coldness about them even in the middle of summer. Mother did her best to cheer the place by having a huge open fire in the living room. Next to it was a big, old-fashioned, black oven and she did most of her cooking on that rather than in the chilly turret kitchen. The big open fire was the centre of our existence in the cold days—we lived around it, for although we had electric lights there were no sockets, no gas and no other form of heating.

The building between the two archways was used as a centre for estate staff functions, and the building similar to ours on the other side served as quarters for the chauffeurs who lived there when the Royal Family were in residence.

Every day a school bus came from Braemar and picked us up at the end of the road to take us to Ballater School, where I concentrated on French and cookery. Neither my sister nor myself was ever encouraged to work hard at school or attempt anything ambitious as—according to Father—'lassies got married' and there didn't seem to him to be much point in them having a decent education. If I had had the chance, or had been given any encouragement at all, I would like to have been a nurse or something in the field of domestic-science teaching. But apart from the fact that 'lassies got married', higher education of any kind still had to be paid for in those days and Father couldn't even have considered that on a wage of £3.50 a week.

At the side of our house was a big shed where Father did a lot of his work. In it, tucked away at the back, was an old closed carriage with wooden wheels, shafts for the horses and rich, red upholstery worn with the years. My brother and I—he was just a toddler—used to have great fun jumping in and out of the funny old carriage, playing at lords and ladies or cowboys and Indians depending on my mood at the time. We were honoured children indeed. The carriage in which we had many an hour of childish fun was the one in which Queen Victoria was driven back and forward to Crathie Church when she was in residence at Balmoral.

The honour of playing in Queen Victoria's old carriage didn't make up for the distinct loneliness of the estate children. There weren't many other youngsters around to play with and I did experience a feeling of being cut off from the rest of the world when I walked from the school bus through the great gates at the end of the day.

My parents had always drummed into me that Balmoral was a royal home and that visiting royalty were entitled to privacy. I should never, under any circumstances, be a 'Peeping Tom'. It was hard, however, to avoid the Royal Family. You were never sure when you turned a corner that you wouldn't bump into one of them—and because we lived so near the castle I often encountered the Queen and

Princesses on the surrounding walks or driveways, either walking with their dogs or on horseback.

If I caught a glimpse of any of them in time I would discreetly change my direction or make a quick detour through the trees to give them the privacy they deserved. In any case, I was always rather shy of meeting them—and I felt awkward having to curtsy on a pathway, sometimes with a school-bag on my back and looking untidy after a day at school!

One side of our house skirted the driveway leading from the front of the Castle to the garages and to the stables where the young princesses kept their horses. The two of them used to walk past down to the stables regularly every morning, and it was amusing to see them dressed in baggy, creased trousers, battered-looking raincoats and old headscarves while the house guests who accompanied them were always immaculately turned-out in the most expensively-tailored riding habits! The young Princess Elizabeth was always the more solemn and serious-looking. Princess Margaret was always laughing, joking with her guests and radiating a happy, vivacious personality.

I was about fourteen or fifteen when I first became aware of the budding romance between Princess Margaret and Peter Townsend, the King's equerry. In fact everyone on the estate knew about it, but very little was said or gossiped about the two young people who seemed to find so much joy in one another's company.

Princess Margaret simply radiated happiness. I would see her often, walking around the stables escorted by Peter Townsend. Sometimes she would be dressed in a kilt and sweater, sometimes in windcheater and slacks. He was always immaculate, of course, and a very handsome man. I often met him on his own as he cycled around the estate. He always greeted me with a friendly 'good morning' or 'good afternoon', as he did everyone who lived at Balmoral.

I remember saying to my mother that perhaps Princess Margaret and Peter Townsend were in love, but I was promptly warned not to speak of such things. My mother's words, however, didn't stop me sensing the growing relationship, or thinking about it. No two people who looked into one another's eyes the way they did, no young man and woman parting from one another with such slow lingering steps and meeting again with such a glow of happiness could be anything else but in love with each other, and secretly I felt very happy for both of them.

Little did I realise then the far-reaching repercussions that can result from a man and woman simply being in love.

My very first long evening dress was a simple one of pale-blue taffeta, with a high neckline and a gathered waist. I wore it when I accompanied my parents to the annual Ghillies' Ball at the Castle.

This was the first time I had been to an occasion when the Royal Family entertained the estate tenants. The Scottish Dance band played on the ballroom balcony and the assembled tenants were joined by a party of kilted soldiers in full evening dress.

Soon, the doors at the head of the ballroom stairs opened and King George, wearing the kilt, and Queen Elizabeth, a tartan sash over her ivory-coloured evening gown, descended the stairs. They were closely followed by the two Princesses, the Duchess of Kent, the Duke and Duchess of Gloucester, Princess Alexandra and many other members of the Royal Family and guests.

When the music began the Royals swept on to the floor and the evening of dancing began. After waltzes, quadrilles and eightsome reels a Paul Jones was announced. I was standing in the circle waiting for the music to begin when a gloved hand slipped into mine. On turning round I looked into the eyes of Princess Margaret, tiny and slim with her tartan sash flowing in the air behind her as she danced.

I left Ballater School when I was fifteen. My mother had already spoken to the Castle housekeeper about the possibility of getting a job as her assistant, and I was accepted for the post. This meant I had to live inside the castle, in a little bedroom decorated mainly in pine with a small bed, a wardrobe and a big, old-fashioned dressing table. Early every morning I had to trudge down to the cellar and carry pails of coal up the steep steps to the housekeeper's own apartment, where I set the fire. The apartment then had to be cleaned and polished to perfection for the housekeeper, a tall, slim, kindly woman in her fifties.

I only had one Sunday afternoon off every second week, and one afternoon off in the middle of the other week. I was kept working pretty hard, and in what little spare time I had I was told to help the sewing maid in the sewing room.

There was a strict class-structure amongst the servants as well as among everyone else. It was rather like a large-scale version of the TV series *Upstairs, Downstairs*. The footmen close to the Royals were the snootiest of all and I, a lowly assistant housekeeper, would never have dreamt of speaking to any of them—had I ever met them! They were almost as remote as the King and Queen themselves.

One morning the housekeeper slept in and I decided to take her breakfast in bed, thinking I was doing well and it would be a kindness she would appreciate. But as things turned out, I put my foot in it. I walked confidently into her room with the breakfast tray to see her sitting up in bed wearing a funny sort of cap. It was very obvious that during the day she wore a wig! Now she knew that I knew. But I think we came to a silent agreement that the subject would never be mentioned.

The housekeeper was a kind woman. I was now learning to bake and make cakes, and she encouraged me and told me I had the makings of an excellent cook.

I was perfectly free to walk into the royal quarters, at any time when the Family weren't in residence, and see the inner splendour of the Castle. A lot of the furniture was covered by dust sheets, but some was visible—and I could always look at the magnificent pictures on the walls. There was pinewood everywhere. I can still remember the smell of it, fresh and clean.

Working in the Castle had its creepy side. There was a strange old woman called Bella Mitchell who 'did' the King's apartments when he was in residence. She talked to herself constantly, and at nights as I sat up in bed reading I could hear her chattering away in her room upstairs.

Only once did I get a quick glimpse of the royal table set for dinner. It was magnificent with its candles and silver. But although we never ate at any royal table, we certainly got a taste of royal food. Every year a French pastry chef came from London to create delicacies for his famous gourmets, and his wife used to stay with my family. Each day he would bring my mother some of his creations, delicious pastries and cream cakes or jellied chicken pies he made for the shooting parties. The deer house was only a stone's throw away from ours, and my family were given pails of venison—which was cooked and eaten immediately. There was no fridge in those days!

One memorable day I was one of a dozen women invited to tea with Her Majesty. It was a special occasion, to thank us for the gift of an elaborately-embroidered tablecloth for the royal household. I had done my share of the embroidery, and so I was included among the Queen's guests. I was introduced to her as the girl who had some time previously played the part of Queen Victoria in a local childrens' pageant, and she smiled graciously and said 'I hear playing the part didn't turn your head!'

We were then taken into the ballroom and the royal nanny brought in a tiny Prince Charles, dressed in a romper-suit. The mischievous toddler proceeded to tug at his grandmother's pearls before he was whisked away again! Then it was up to the royal apartment for afternoon tea—a great privilege indeed. All the ladies present were trying to be terribly polite and were making a great fuss over which of the delicious cakes to choose. I never let them suspect, of course, that the cakes on the trays were the very same as the ones the French pastry chef brought my mother every day! I chose my favourite, a cream bun topped with chopped almonds.

The little tea party lasted about thirty minutes. I remember the Queen herself as a charming woman with a warm personality, who chatted generally to the twelve of us rather than to anyone in particular. It was all very informal, as we enjoyed our cakes and sipped tea from the delicate china cups.

Some time later I met the King at a staff fancy-dress

dance, to which I went as 'Red Tape', wearing a costume covered with anti-Government slogans and protests about income tax. The King was very amused at the idea and came over and told me to turn around so he could read the slogans on the back. He certainly seemed to like my outfit, but although he was one of the judges I didn't win a prize.

The Royal Family had their own private film shows at Balmoral. Both the films and the projectionist were flown specially from London to provide the entertainment. Staff who worked in the Castle were allowed to attend, and if we wanted to get a good seat at the back of the ballroom we could go in half an hour before the film was due to begin. Eventually the Royals would arrive, in full evening dress after their family dinner. They would smile at us, then sit down to await the start of the latest London film. It was nice to have them all smile at us as they entered the ballroom, but soon the novelty wore off. For a young girl like myself the overriding concern was that they should get seated so that we could see the film.

Although I was working as assistant housekeeper I was being trained at the same time as a lady's maid and I suppose that had I remained at Balmoral and made it my career I could have ended up at Buckingham Palace itself. My parents were consequently annoyed and upset when, after only three months at the castle in that job, I decided to leave. I had no intention of being 'shut away' from the world in a place like that for the rest of my life, for I could well have ended up like the funny old lady who 'did' the King's apartments . . . talking to myself. I felt there was much more to life—and I wanted to learn about it. It was 1950. My mother was recovering from a serious operation and I went home to look after my father and brother while she was in hospital. When she was allowed home I got a job in Aberdeen—as a clerkess in an agency for taxis and buses. The pay was £2 a week, which was more than double what I had been getting in my job at the Castle. I enjoyed my busy new life—so different from the seclusion of the Balmoral estate.

I stayed with that firm for nearly a year, and by the time I applied for another job—with a coal and shipping agency—

I was almost seventeen. In the meantime the family had moved back to Stonehaven. I travelled back and forward to Aberdeen by train.

I was just seventeen when I met the first love of my life, at a dance in Stonehaven. He was only a little older than I was and we went out together for a year. Nothing is quite like your first love: it can never be repeated and things are never the same with anyone else. I will never forget him. After twelve months' courtship, however, he broke it off—and like most other starry-eyed teenagers it took me quite a while and a lot of tears to get over him.

Then one Saturday night in January 1953, I went to a dance in Stonehaven Town Hall with one of my girl friends. I was eighteen and I remember I was wearing a blue dress that evening.

Dances in small towns do not offer much variety—the same faces turn up at each one. You get tired of dancing with the same local lads. But on this evening two strangers suddenly appeared at the door; two young men I had never seen before. One of them, tall and dark-haired in a smart suit, looked rather nice.

The next dance was a ladies' choice.

Like many a youngster on such an occasion, I thought 'What have I got to lose?' I asked him to dance. . . . Right in the middle of the number he stopped, took out his handkerchief and blew his nose! I thought it was rather a funny thing to do. To me it indicated that there was something different about him.

When the dance ended, he took me to the refreshment area for a cup of tea and introduced himself.

'My name is Max. Max Garvie.' He smiled. 'What's yours?'

3

There was an immediate attraction between Max Garvie and me. I felt completely at ease that night in Stonehaven Town Hall as we chatted over a cup of tea, and he seemed the sort of man who would be easy to get along with. The talk, naturally, turned to farming and it turned out he knew a relative of mine who ran a farm near Edzell. He told me with great enthusiasm that he was doing a course of farming in Aberdeen, where he lived in digs.

He was charming, and as the evening wore on we danced more closely, like any other young couple who had just met and between whom there was an obvious attraction. When the dance ended and it was time to head for home, Max, his friend, myself and my girl friend—who was staying the night at my parents' home in Stonehaven—piled into Max's little Morris car.

Max and I lingered behind. He kissed me good night— just a simple 'peck on the cheek'—and asked if I would go out with him the following Wednesday. I agreed, and walked into the house feeling just an inch or two above the ground. It was a good feeling to have a date with a nice young man.

He picked me up that Wednesday evening and we headed for the cinema—to watch *Limelight*, I remember, starring Charlie Chaplin and Claire Bloom. In the darkened cinema Max put his arm around me and there were a few, first real kisses. Then, the perfect gentleman, he drove me home.

Our relationship was established very quickly. We would go out twice or three times a week, dancing, to the cinema or for a drink. All the time we were together I knew that we would soon have to part, for in the spring he was leaving for a farm in Norfolk to do a year's practical course as part of his training. Only three months after we met, Max headed south.

Absence, however, did in this case make both hearts grow fonder, and our relationship was strong enough to survive the long separation. We wrote to each other regularly—twice a week—and while he was away I never went out with anyone else. Those letters were far from passionate on either side. His were mostly about farming and how much he was enjoying learning the practical side of the business; mine were just general chit-chat about what was happening to myself, my family and the mutual friends we had made during our three months' courtship.

Once a week Max telephoned. I looked forward each time to the chatty long-distance calls. In addition, three or four times during that year he came up for long weekends and once I went down for a short holiday—only a week—and stayed in a little hotel in Norfolk. That was wonderful and it was great to be with him again. My parents never objected to me going off on my own to see Max. I suppose they trusted me and presumed that my puritanical upbringing would ensure I didn't 'step out of line'. But in fact it was during that week in the Norfolk countryside that Max and I were first intimate.

He came back north for good in the spring of 1954 and it seemed natural that we should start talking about when we would get engaged. I thought the world of him then. I deeply respected him and had a great admiration for his intellect and business brain. A deep, passionate love, however—for me at least—it was not. I had been very much in love before and I had made up my mind that I would never be hurt again.

All of our dates, everything we did and everywhere we went, was planned by Max. I had little say in anything. Nevertheless, our dates were fun. He was generous and enjoyed a good time, which usually by this time meant having quite a lot to drink. I enjoyed the cinema, but Max preferred to go to a Saturday night dance, or drink with friends in local cocktail bars. His drinking didn't really worry me, because although he took a fair amount of liquor he never seemed to get drunk.

I had never been involved with alcohol before, but by this time I was being encouraged to have a few drinks on a night out, usually a mixture of dark rum and orange juice. There had never been drink in my home—my parents never drank—and I would always go home at night terrified that they would smell it on my breath. I knew if they did there would be a row. I ate a lot of peppermint sweets in those days. . . .

The only boy I had ever introduced to my father was a little friend at school, aged eight. He had asked my father if he could buy me for £100! But as Christmas 1954 drew closer it was obvious that soon Max would have to meet the head of my family. He had never been inside the house, for when he arrived to take me out he would stop his car in the road outside and toot his horn. When he brought me home he would simply say the usual 'good nights' and drive away—without venturing any closer to my home than the door at the bottom of the garden.

One Saturday afternoon he said he must come back and meet my father because he wanted to ask him if he could marry me. We were both a bit nervous, but we went boldly into the house and found Father sitting in the living room reading a newspaper. I introduced Max, they exchanged a few pleasantries and small talk, then Father promptly started reading again with even more concentration than before.

It was all rather embarrassing. Max hedged a bit, then came straight out with it. 'Mr Watson, I want to marry Sheila.'

Father looked up and replied 'Well, it that's what you want then it's up to yourselves.' It was obvious he approved, in his own stern way.

Mother said very little about the whole thing—certainly nothing against Max—but on the other hand she didn't seem too enthusiastic.

Looking back, I think now that the fact that Max came from a wealthy farming family and that their younger daughter was clearly making a good match coloured my parents' opinion of him. In any case it was just quietly accepted that we were going to be engaged, then married, and that was that.

At Christmas, Max's parents invited us both to a dance in Edzell and I knew that his mother was anxious for him to announce our engagement during the evening in front of all her friends. But he didn't. The evening wore on, the couples danced and the drinks flowed without any indication from Max that he was going to tell the assembled company of his engagement to Sheila Watson.

The dance ended; we left and drove off into the night. On a quiet stretch of road, Max stopped the car and did the only really romantic thing he ever did in all the years we were together. Slipping a diamond ring on my finger, he told me quietly he wanted to get engaged this way—just the two of us together—instead of in front of all those people. I was thrilled. It was wonderful to have a ring on my finger—three diamonds—and I was starry-eyed at the way he had done it.

By this time Max was staying at our future home, the farmhouse of West Cairnbeg, and it was decided we would get married the following summer. My family didn't have enough money to splash out on a big white wedding with a lavish reception, so our second decision was that our marriage would be small and quiet. Max had readily agreed, saying 'I've been to lots of big posh weddings and never enjoyed any of them.'

I was a member of Dunnottar Church, near Stonehaven (and a Sunday School teacher there) so six weeks before the wedding we went to see the minister to make the arrangements. I don't believe he made any impression on Max as Max wasn't religious in any way.

I didn't have a show of presents, as was customary in our area, for I didn't want to have people trailing around the house, putting my mother to a lot of trouble. In any case, I never liked the idea of showing off wedding gifts—as if you were smugly saying 'Look what I've got!' I remember, however, two of my presents in particular—a very expensive, beautiful coffee set which was later used at special dinner-parties at the farm, and a magnificent wrought-iron standard lamp which stood at the top of the staircase at West Cairnbeg.

Max and I were married at midday on 11 June 1955. Like every other bride I was out of bed at the crack of dawn, wondering nervously if everything would run smoothly. Until half an hour before leaving the house I was still writing the last of the 'thank you' letters to people who had sent presents. Just before we left for the church by taxi my father poured me a large glass of sherry to calm my nerves. It was the first drink he had ever given me.

I wore a deep royal-blue suit with matching shoes and handbag and a pale-blue blouse and floppy hat. It was the first time in my life I had ever worn a hat, and I can't remember wearing one since. I don't like hats.

I had shared all my pre-wedding preparations, tears and nerves with a good friend of mine, Emily Milne, and I wanted her to be my best maid. But somehow things went wrong and it was silently agreed amongst everyone else that Max's sister would be best maid.

There were ten of us at the church; the bridal couple, my parents, Max's parents, the best man George Still, Max's sister, my friend Emily and my young brother William, then aged eleven. With the minister and his wife, the wedding party swelled to twelve. Max was his usual jovial self, despite the fact that he'd had a rip-roaring stag night the night before. It had ended at a party with some of his farming friends near Aberdeen. Nevertheless, he and the best man had already enjoyed a few more drinks in a Stonehaven hotel before they arrived at the church.

What followed was not a happy wedding day.

I'll never know what kind of premonition my mother had that day, but just as the minister started to give us his blessing, she began to weep. There was I, a starry-eyed bride of twenty, standing beside my groom admiring the gold band on my finger when suddenly I heard my mother crying.

I turned to give her a smile, thinking she was shedding the sort of tears that every mother cries at a daughter's wedding, but her eyes did not reflect any joy. Far from it. She was a ghastly white, like someone who has suffered a shock, and she was gripping the front of the pew desperately with both hands. I gave Father a meaningful look and turned my attention back to what the minister was saying, but I couldn't help wondering if she'd been taken ill.

She had cheered up, however, by the time the little wedding party reached the Bay Hotel in Stonehaven where we had booked a small function room for the wedding lunch. Max laughed it off by saying 'Cheer up, Mrs Watson. Sons-in-law like me don't come along every day!'

I joked too. 'I hope there were none of your "spookies" at my wedding, Mum!' My mother was a keen spiritualist all her life and I often used to tease her about her 'spookies'.

Despite these little jokes, however, the atmosphere remained strained. Mrs Garvie was sitting next to the minister with whom she obviously wasn't getting along, and I think my parents both felt rather uncomfortable in the presence of the wealthy Garvies.

There was a choice of fruit juice or soup, salmon or steak and there was no wine with the meal. Father made a short speech and so did Max. I remember very little about either of them. We were out of the Bay Hotel by two o'clock. The guests dispersed, but before Max and I left, Max's mother presented him with a parcel containing a pair of green and white silk pyjamas.

My wedding was over—and I was glad. It was not a particularly happy day and I doubt if any of us really enjoyed it.

There was one odd thing that I couldn't get out of my mind. Six weeks before we were married, Max's mother had told him about a farmer's son whose wife had contracted TB a few weeks after they were married. Max had insisted I should have a full check-up at the doctor's before our wedding. The incident preyed on my mind for a long time, although I don't know why. It seemed rather an odd thing for a prospective groom to ask of his bride-to-be.

The two of us drove out of Stonehaven in the little Morris car, heading south for Edinburgh on the first stage of our honeymoon. Max, as usual, had arranged everything and we spent our wedding night in a big comfortable double room in the Carlton Hotel. Sex with Max wasn't completely strange to me, but our wedding night was nevertheless a passionate one.

After breakfast we headed for the airport and flew to

London. It was the very first time I had ever been in an aircraft and I was absolutely terrified. The only good thing about our flight south was that I wasn't sick! We stayed one night in London, then flew on to Majorca where we were booked in for two weeks at the Oasis Hotel, three miles outside Palma.

We spent long lazy days relaxing in the sun, swimming and enjoying the beauty of the place. I was very thrilled about my first trip abroad and couldn't believe anywhere could be so hot. I suffered the usual sunburn and 'Spanish tummy' and remember disliking the heavy, greasy food.

Max hired a scooter and we had a lot of fun touring parts of the island. I think Max got bored just sitting around. He always wanted to be on the move. He was happy as a lark tearing about on the scooter.

Max had already been abroad—to Scandinavia to see some new farming methods—and he found it easy to chat to foreigners and the strangers we met. I, on the other hand, was shy and found it difficult to strike up conversations with people I had never met before. Max scolded me for not talking to people enough. Why was I so shy and reticent? Why couldn't I join in like everyone else? He was annoyed because I wasn't as extrovert and out-going with people as he was. Even when we were still on our way to Majorca, I had been lost and confused by London Airport—and Max had been more annoyed than helpful.

On our honeymoon I also discovered that Max regarded sex as purely for his own satisfaction and never seemed to bother whether I had enjoyed our love-making or not. He was only interested in his own needs and reactions and had a distinct lack of feeling towards mine. Even before we were married, he had given me sex textbooks to read, with the result that I felt completely ignorant, stupid and out of my depth right from the start. I could only hope that things would improve.

After our two weeks in the sun we left Majorca to return to the Mearns and our new home at West Cairnbeg.

It was a grand farmhouse in a lovely setting, surrounded

by acres of crops ripening in the flaming red soil of which the Mearns folk are so proud. I looked forward to my new life with enthusiasm—and optimism that Max and I would share it with happiness. I must have been the envy of many a young single girl in the area, for I had married a handsome, clever, wealthy young farmer and was about to start married life in a lovely home. The big glass porch at West Cairnbeg led on to a spacious hallway, off which were the lounge, dining room and kitchen, and a maid's room which had been converted into an office. Upstairs were four bedrooms and a bathroom.

In the few months that followed I tried very hard to settle into the new way of life, both at West Cairnbeg and in the Mearns farming community. The hustle and bustle of my busy office in Aberdeen seemed very distant. I felt like a plant which had been uprooted and re-bedded amongst a strange and foreign variety. Max was kind, considerate and tolerant of my moods then, but failed to understand the loneliness I was experiencing. He was unable to grasp that I could feel such an intangible isolation amid the comfort and security he had provided for me. It was as if I was casting a long, lingering look behind at a familiar door that had closed on me, and was filled with uncertainty about what lay beyond the door that stood open before me.

I missed the warmth and friendliness of my old family home and the close-knit family atmosphere in which I had been brought up. It had been a working-class home without airs, graces or sophistication: there had been no fine house and sumptuous furnishings, but neither had there been any notions of grandeur. I had never lived on a 'showpiece' farm before and I was on the go from morning till night cleaning, polishing and keeping the place shining for the visitors who kept appearing unannounced.

The first shades of disillusionment which had begun to cloud the intimate side of our marriage on our honeymoon now grew darker. There was none of the romanticism I had hoped for, just cold-blooded, unemotional sex that gradually numbed my physical senses.

Max was a clever young man, a good farmer full of new

ideas, and he was away a lot in the evenings talking to agricultural committees and meetings, both nearby and much further afield. I was terribly proud of him and gave him all the help and encouragement I could. Often I was his sole audience and critic before he set out to deliver a speech or lecture to a group of farmers. There were some weeks, however, when he didn't spend one single evening at home and during those lonely hours at West Cairnbeg my only companion was a big, floppy Labrador dog which Max had bought for me.

We socialised and entertained on a scale that befitted our status in the Mearns community. Max was chairman of the Fettercairn Young Farmers Club and involved in other farming organisations. There were social events and dinner dances to attend fairly regularly.

I did my best to fit in with the other farmers' wives, all rooted perennials of respectability, participating in their 'events' and accepting and offering invitations to coffee mornings and tea parties—which I later grew to hate. The society contained all sorts of class subdivisions depending on one's farming 'pedigree' and material wealth. At the coffee mornings and the tea parties the talk revolved around families and the problems of getting staff; the gossip was all about wives who weren't present and any hint of local scandal sparked off hours of chit-chat.

I was accepted by the exclusive élite because Max's family had farmed at West Cairnbeg for generations—sowing the seeds of social discrimination—and they had money. Snobbery was rife. Although a high proportion of this farming community seemed poorly-educated, big farms and big money gave them a high status in the community.

I was confident, however, in the knowledge that I was good at managing the household affairs and at entertaining Max's friends and associates. I knew my 'spreads' were just as good, if not better, than anyone else's and I never felt inferior when the ladies of the community arrived for afternoon tea or some of Max's friends came for dinner at night.

Sometimes, indeed, the behaviour of members of this so-called 'élite' shocked me. The very first Hogmanay we spent at West Cairnbeg a band of young farmers arrived for their New Year drinks. They were all, quite literally, out of their minds with drink. They poured spirits and beer on the floor, stubbed their cigarettes out on the carpet and smashed expensive crystal glasses without a thought. One very prominent Mearns farmer squirted the contents of a soda syphon all over the walls—and Max didn't bother one bit. He regarded it all as a big joke.

I didn't feel in a position to complain. It was Max's family who had taken charge of the furnishings and decoration of the farmhouse, and I had had no say in the matter at all. I was never able to choose my living-room suite, or the colour of my curtains. It was all done without even asking my advice. In many ways I felt like a stranger in my own home. Cleaning, cooking and entertaining hordes of guests at the drop of a hat, I felt, reduced me often to the level of a servant, and I was reminded of my three months in Balmoral Castle.

I was a member of a little book club which met once a month to order and exchange books; members were mostly local farmers' wives and the meetings were largely used as a chance for yet another gossip session.

When the books were published we all chose a title and exchanged it with someone else at the next meeting. One night, just to be rebellious, I picked *No Adam in Eden* by Grace Metalious—the author of *Peyton Place*. Everyone was slightly shocked but they all read it just the same! Often Max used to choose my titles for me because he thought some of the spicier novels would shock all those straightlaced farmers' wives and cause a few blushes. There was such an atmosphere of hypocrisy! On the face of it they were all prudes but they loved to get hold of a juicy book or hear about a bit of neighbourhood scandal. The talk would keep them going for days on end.

In the autumn of 1955 I suspected I was pregnant and a visit to the local doctor in Laurencekirk confirmed that I was expecting a child.

I was delighted. Max was pleased, but he was no warmer

towards me than he'd been at any time before. Being in an advanced state of pregnancy didn't absolve me from my daily obligations of cooking and entertaining farming friends of Max's and I found it very embarrassing to carry trays of food in to a roomful of men when I was heavily pregnant.

Louise was born in the early summer of 1956, in the middle of the night in a private nursing home. Max arrived the next day awkwardly clutching a bunch of flowers, obviously the first flowers he had ever bought for anyone. There were two daffodils, a couple of carnations and two roses. Louise was in a cot by my bedside and Max was obviously very pleased with himself as a father—although, like many men, I think he would have preferred a son.

Only four months later I got a real shock when I discovered I was pregnant again. Eleven months after Louise's birth, Claire made her appearance in the world. It was an extra strain, of course, looking after the two babies and all the guests as well, but Max agreed to employ a full time maid to help me, and the burden was eased. As the girls grew older, I took them for walks in the surrounding countryside, exploring Nature in all her many facets. We tramped over grassy hills and carpets of wild flowers, jumped over streamy ditches, paddled and splashed in the burns. A picnic was always the highlight of our adventurous afternoons. Then, on the way home, Louise and Claire would gather bunches of wild flowers for me, and our home was full of their posies. Those were happy days.

In the summer of 1959 we drove down to the South of France with the two little girls and had a wonderful, three-week camping holiday. It was my first time abroad since our honeymoon and I enjoyed so much watching the youngsters having the time of their lives in the warm sunshine.

In the spring of the following year Max suggested we do the same thing again, drive down to the beautiful Côte d'Azur and repeat the happy experiences of our first trip.

I was delighted to think that once again we would all be together in that lovely part of the world, and I thought it would be another wonderful holiday.

I was to be proved wrong.

4

We drove south to the sun, myself, Max, Louise and Claire.

We basked on the sun-bleached beaches near fashionable St Tropez, we swam and we spent many days exploring the glorious coastline of the South of France. I felt relaxed and happy. I loved to see my two daughters playing in the sun, laughing and giggling together. I revelled in the scenery and enjoyed the fragrant, balmy scents of the exotic shrubs and flowers which fringe those Mediterranean shores.

One day we found ourselves in the tiny port of Le Lavandou, a picturesque little place about thirty miles east of Toulon. We pottered around the harbour—and suddenly Max drew my attention to a sign placed discreetly at one end of the bay. Nearby was moored a small, white-painted ferry, and on the quayside a weatherbeaten seafaring man appeared to be selling tickets for some kind of excursion. Max became very excited and declared that we should all embark for the next sailing in ten minutes' time.

The sign was printed in French, of course, and gave details of times of departure to and return from the Ile du Levant, a place I had never heard of before but—as it turned out—a place I shall never forget. I looked closer, saw the words '*Réserve Naturiste*' and exclaimed to Max 'Louise and Claire would love that! Will they be able to feed the birds?' I thought it was some kind of nature reserve.

Max burst into fits of uncontrollable laughter. Finally, he managed to explain. 'I wouldn't bother about the birds. This place is strictly for nudists!'

I was speechless.

'Come on, let's go and look it over,' Max said, grinning.

I couldn't believe my ears! I managed, however, to blurt out that I didn't have the slightest inclination to see any such place and certainly no intention of going there, especially since the children were with us. I was panic-stricken. My first thoughts were for the two little girls—Louise was four and Claire three—and what effect the things they might see on this island could have upon them.

My reply, however, fell on deaf ears and further angry protests from me were similarly disregarded. Within seconds Max had parked the car and had whisked the two girls out of it, and the three of them were running along the quayside towards the white boat and the ticket-seller. As he ran, Max shouted over his shoulder to me to be sure the car doors were locked and to remember to bring the keys. Hesitantly, and slightly bewildered, I followed his instructions. I joined them as they were about to go on board with about another twenty passengers. Within a few minutes the little ferry had left the harbour and was setting its course for the Ile du Levant.

Louise and Claire skipped around the deck, full of fun and high spirits and obviously delighted that a boat trip was to be included in the day's outing. Max was in a high good humour and kept congratulating himself that he had remembered, in the rush to catch the ferry, to bring his camera equipment from the car. He strutted around the deck reloading the cameras and explaining to me that visitors and sightseers were welcome on the island and that I was stupid to be so straightlaced and prudish. He was highly amused by my obvious embarrassment and treated my reaction to the prospect of visiting the nudist colony as a huge joke.

The fact that I was being ferried to a nudist island had stripped me of all conversation. Apart from a superficial, secretive, school-rude knowledge of nudism, I had not the remotest idea what I would find on this island. Max was the only man I had ever seen naked. I could not remember ever seeing my own mother or father in even a partial state of undress and I had not seen my brother or sister naked since we were children together.

I had been brought up in the firm belief that the acts of dressing, undressing and bathing were always to be performed in privacy and seclusion behind closed doors. This was an observance that was treated with respect in our family; a part of living I had accepted without question. Nakedness, for me, was a private thing. Like sex, it was something experienced in the intimate situation between husband and wife. The thought of people displaying themselves in the nude in public appalled me.

As the little ferry boat forged towards the island I tried to console myself with the thought that perhaps its inhabitants would be well screened from visiting tourists. Probably the nudists would be confined to an area excluded from the prying eyes of sightseers. . . .

On first sight the Ile du Levant looked barren and rocky, but as we drew closer I could see thickly-wooded areas and groves of bushy ferns which grew in hollows beyond the rocky fringe. Men and women thronged the small jetty and gathered on the wooden landing-stage as the boat drew alongside. This sun-tanned group was clutching suitcases and bags and was—to my great relief—fully-clothed. I looked around furtively, but apart from the people ready to board the ferry there was no-one in sight. The area round the jetty was completely deserted.

As we stepped ashore I quietly took Louise and Claire aside, for I knew I would have to explain to them somehow.

'There are people on this island who like to lie in the sunshine without wearing any clothes. If you see any of them, you must not point fingers or laugh.' It was the best I could think of. I was relieved to think that the two girls had spent all their young lives on a farm surrounded by animals and had had a more 'down-to-earth' upbringing than myself. I hoped and prayed that if we did come across any of the nudists, Louise and Claire would not bother about them.

As for Max, his face fell the moment we stepped ashore. Right in front of us was a large notice in four languages stating categorically that the use of cameras on the island was strictly forbidden and that on no account must tourists take any pictures. He was furious. I realised that there was nothing he would have liked better than to photograph the nudists—and his plans to do so had been foiled!

Another sign—arrow-shaped, and displaying the word 'Village'—pointed towards a path leading away from the jetty.

It was was now past midday. Louise and Claire were obviously getting hungry and Max was certain that in this village there would be a hotel or restaurant in which we could have something to eat. There was no transport, so the four of us set off to walk along the track in the hot sun. I noticed that our fellow passengers were now scattered about the rocky paths.

The track led us through avenues of pine trees with downward-sloping branches which sheltered us, thankfully, from the blazing midday sun. We had just turned a bend when I saw a man about ten yards away and walking towards us. I almost exclaimed out loud 'Good Heavens, it's Rip Van Winkle himself!'

He was an old man, slightly stooped, with a shock of long white hair cascading over his shoulders and his chestnut-coloured skin the texture of baked leather. His body, though shrunken, was lean and sinewy and completely unclothed—except for a long, silvery-white beard which reached almost to his navel.

Smothering his laughter, Max put his finger to his lips, lowered his eyebrows and shook his head as if to tell us not to say anything.

After the aged nudist had passed I looked anxiously at the two girls, and was filled immediately with a sense of relief as I saw them hopping excitedly from foot to foot and whispering childishly 'Mummy, did you see that man's long beard?' I nodded my head in assent and they skipped away laughing and singing, as if our encounter with 'Rip Van Winkle' was an everyday occurrence.

After ten minutes' walk I caught my first glimpse of the village, which consisted of clusters of artistic little log cabins secluded among clumps of trees and tangled shrubbery. There were naked people walking around the buildings and among the trees. I wanted to turn and run, but my worry and disquiet were swamped by Max's glowing enthusiasm for our new, strange surroundings. His eyes followed the naked sun-worshippers everywhere and I knew he would have loved to have been able to record the scene on his camera.

We lunched in a small hotel nearby. Our fellow diners were all naked. They drifted to and fro carrying handbags and cushions or sat around casually eating and drinking; the young, the old, the fat, the thin, the attractive, the ugly. Fortunately the children were hungry enough to concentrate more on their meal than on their strange dining companions, but I for my part was nervous and embarrassed and simply wanted to finish lunch and get out of the place as fast as possible.

Then came another blow.

'Let's take our clothes off and join them,' suggested Max, grinning. 'There's no reason to be a prude!'

A chilling shock pierced me. I felt trapped, as if my body was about to be violated. My reaction was one of disgust and repulsion. I told him that he could forget the idea. Nothing would persuade me to undress, and under no circumstances would I allow the girls to do so either. I was determined and Max was angry. We finished lunch and headed back along the path to the jetty. The ferry took us ashore and the end of the holiday was in sight. This year, I was glad.

Back at West Cairnbeg, and back in the routine of everyday life on the farm, I gradually began to forget that miserable day on the nudist island, although it had shaken me to the core. Once again, we were absorbed into the communal life of the neighbourhood: the socialising, the visits to agricultural shows. I was pulled back into the rounds of coffee mornings and afternoon teas.

Although I entertained with confidence, I was never sufficiently interested to compete with other wives in the jam-and-sponge-making scene at the local shows. I could not be persuaded that it was a vital part of the role of wife and mother to spend hours studying the hydrodynamics and technology of advanced jam-making or debating whether the addition of another egg would fluff my sponge cake higher than Mrs So-and-So's. The samples of culinary genius entered in those local contests were spectacular, but how on earth the judges managed to decide whose jam was best after tasting countless specimens of the same variety and appearance was beyond my understanding.

We saw little of Max on these occasions. He directed his energies into organising sports events—marking out the course for the Grannies' Race or using the power of carrot-bait to spur on the donkeys! But by the late summer of 1962 Max's fast and furious enthusiasm for these amusements had slowed to a bored canter. I could sense his unrest. The wind of change, like the approaching autumn, was blowing in our direction.

The storm broke one evening as we sat by the fireside in the lounge at West Cairnbeg, just the two of us. The children were in bed.

Max's words dropped like a bombshell.

'We must join a nudist club,' he said.

He told me how important and necessary it was that I should give my full agreement to the plan, and my absolute cooperation. Unknown to me he had already been in touch with a nudist club secretary, and had been told that they preferred married couples as members rather than single people.

I tried to cut my way through to him, appealing to his love, his sympathy, his understanding. I begged him to consider my feelings and pleaded to be spared this unreasonable duress. But Max was determined. We were to join the club and that was that. He declared that my birth and upbringing had wedded me to old-fashioned ideas that nowadays meant nothing. I should discard my crutches and start 'living' in the new, permissive age.

Later, in bed beside him, I lay awake in a turmoil of emotion. I was beginning to realise that I was married to a man who, despite his wealth, status, mastery of farming and intelligence, was rich only in material things. To Max, I was just another of his possessions. And he was becoming gradually perverted. Not only was he developing an unhealthy interest in nudism, but he was starting to make abnormal sexual demands on me. They were demands with which I simply could not cope. It was the first real crisis in my life.

Having finally fallen asleep, I awoke the next morning with a mixture of feelings for Max—pity, love and sorrow. I knew that he lacked profundity of feeling, but I still retained a great loyalty towards the man I had married and whose children I had borne. So I realised that this time there was no way out—I would have to comply with his wishes. Reluctantly, I told him I would join the club. Reluctantly, I agreed I would go with him. But turning over the new, glossy page in that chapter of my life was like turning my back on God.

My first impression of Max's nudist club was anaesthetised by the liberal amount of alcohol I had drunk in a hotel we had visited *en route*. I had enjoyed a few drinks with Max during our courtship, and thereafter had taken the occasional festive glass at social gatherings, but on this occasion I felt I needed something stronger to get me through the most embarrassing day of my life.

The 'club' turned out to be a dilapidated, two-roomed cottage buried in the remote countryside some distance from the main Edinburgh–Newcastle road. It was badly in need of repair and renovation. There was an enclosure of interwoven fencing and tall, trailing trees which offered seclusion and privacy for members. When we arrived that Sunday afternoon several children were playing and spashing about in a home-constructed swimming pool at the end of a grassy 'sunning area' in front of the cottage. To the left was what I later learned was the sauna room but which at first glance looked like a kennel for a large dog.

The club secretary, proprietor, organiser and—it appeared to me—one-man committee was a healthy-looking, bright-eyed, middle-aged man. His wife was the same type: fresh-faced, healthy and tanned. They were obviously both keen on fresh-air and keeping fit, and enthused about the effects of their sauna room—which, they said, restored youth, health and bloom. I didn't like to say that I felt not at all in need of restorative cures. An outdoor life on the farm at West Cairnbeg was a fine recipe for fitness.

We were introduced to another couple about the same ages as ourselves, who had been hovering in the background.

Although I must admit that my eyes were not focusing too clearly that day, I was sober enough to decide that the man had evil-looking eyes. We were all introduced by our first names only and were assured by the 'head man' of the club that although there was only a small group present that day there was in fact a large membership, many of whom could not attend regularly because, like ourselves, they lived a long distance away.

The club's amenities were, to say the least, limited. The sauna room was the main attraction for members. We six adults—the proprietor and his wife, 'evil eyes' and his wife and Max and I—undressed behind a screen in one of the cottage's two rooms. I felt terrible. Clad only in goosepimples and horribly embarrassed I joined the procession to the kennel-like sauna. If it had not been for the number of drinks I had consumed I would probably have turned and run.

Nine naked bodies—six adults and the proprietor's three children—were crammed into the little hut, which was about four feet wide and six feet long. We sat on two wooden benches on either side of a solid-fuel stove.

I noticed with apprehension that 'evil eyes' invited one of the proprietor's little girls to sit on his knee. With relief, my thoughts sped to Stonehaven where I knew my own two little daughters were safely in the care of my mother. She had been told that Max and I were visiting farming friends near Edinburgh.

The heat from the stove was intense and the cottage-owner and his wife started sprinkling something from small bottles on to the hot coals. A sickly odour permeated the already stifling air. I thought my lungs were going to burst. Every nerve and pulse in my body was hammering to get out and I was on the point of collapse when the proprietor saw my predicament and came to the rescue—by opening the door for my hasty exit.

Gasping, I assured him I would be all right, and he went back into the torture chamber. Feeling more dead than alive, I staggered across the grass to the swimming pool and dipped my throbbing head in and out of the water. I was miserable and exhausted. 'Health-giving' they said! Any more of their health treatment would have reduced me to a cremated skeleton.

A good twenty minutes later the rest of them came whooping out of the hut looking like boiled lobsters and plunged into the cool waters of the pool. Max was obviously enjoying every second of his new diversion. Later he told me how invigorated the whole experience had made him feel, both physically and mentally.

Max, of course, was anything but pleased by my first nude performance which was obviously not of the standard he expected from his leading lady. He would have been delighted had I expressed enthusiasm over the visit to the club and would have loved to hear how much I had enjoyed it all. He wanted me to think and act like him and seemed to believe that he could control my reactions and emotions. I wondered how he could possibly want to waste his time with such silly, sordid things. He never saw the unhappiness it caused me, for he was too stagestruck and eager to emulate the other characters in this nudist drama to care how I felt.

At least the visit was over. But I was foolish if I thought it would be the last. A few weeks later I was told we would be going back to the horrible little place.

This time we headed first for Glasgow, where Max bought me a beautiful evening dress costing sixty pounds—a lot of money in those days. But any pleasure I might have got from the dress was ruined by the knowledge that Max was merely trying to 'soften me up' for our second visit to the strange cottage.

There were a few new faces at the club, and all of them— unlike 'evil eyes'—appeared normal enough, but at the very last moment, behind the undressing screens, my courage failed me. I shocked Max by feigning a sore throat and shivery feelings (which were not entirely imaginary). I made my apologies to the others for not undressing and offered to make tea and sandwiches instead of joining them in the sauna.

My suggestion was readily accepted by our fellow members. They were eager for their sauna session, and no doubt it would be handy to have someone tackling the more mundane chores. Max, however, was scowling and silent and I sheltered behind my pretence. He knew very well there was nothing wrong with me.

When he eventually emerged from the pool he was invigorated and pleased with the obvious approval and admiration of the other members. He was certainly a handsome addition to the club. During the long drive home he launched into another scathing attack on my inhibitions, but somehow this time it didn't hurt or worry me so much. I thought that perhaps my excuses were going to work.

My feeling of triumph, however, was short-lived. Once more, it was only a matter of weeks before I was told we were going again. The difference was that this time Louise and Claire were to come with us. . . . My nerves gave way and there was a terrible row. I was at my wits' end trying to think of some way of dissuading him from taking the girls to that place. But the more I shouted, cried, pleaded, the more determined Max became that Louise and Claire were going too. My views were simply swept aside. Once again I was reminded in no uncertain terms of my prudish upbringing and the effect it had had on my attitudes to sex and nudism.

That third visit is vague in my memory. My only thought was to protect my daughters and make sure that no 'evil eyes' came near either of them. I watched their every movement. My fears were allayed by the fact that they lost no time in mixing with the other youngsters and spent most of their time playing in the pool. They appeared unconcerned by the whole situation. But it was cold comfort.

On our return from this third visit I began to worry that one or the other of the girls would innocently say something to my mother, or some other relative or friend. I had nightmares about how my mother would react if one of her grandchildren let it slip that Mummy and Daddy had taken them to a place where the people didn't wear any clothes. I kept putting off visits to my parents' home, making excuses over the telephone that I had a heavy cold, that I was giving the house a clean from top to bottom, that we were busy entertaining.

Then I started to cry. The tears came in floods and bouts

of uncontrollable weeping came without warning, day and night. I wore dark glasses most of the time to hide my red, swollen eyes from the children. I had to force myself to go out shopping, and simple household tasks seemed impossible to tackle. Mornings were the worst times. I would lie weeping in the knowledge that somehow I had to get up and face another day. But night-time was not much better.

A deep depression had set in. Max kept asking what was wrong. He was determined that nothing was going to spoil his new-found pleasures. But I could not answer. My thoughts had become absurd, vague and incomprehensible. I went to our family doctor, who advised me to see a psychiatrist. I really thought I was going mad.

The psychiatrist was a swarthy, dark-haired man who sat behind a wide wooden desk. I told him about my bouts of weeping, my depression and the endless sleepless hours at night. I described the gloom and despair which ended in tears. He threw me a leading question, asking about my sexual relationship with my husband. I tossed the issue back by saying it was 'satisfactory'. He reconnoitred more closely on the subject and I hedged and dodged his pursuit. But how could I tell this total stranger, in whom I had neither trust or confidence, that my husband had taken me and our two daughters to a nudist camp and that his sexual demands were becoming not only excessive, but abnormal and perverted? I thought that if I gave away these secrets to a stranger it could lead to family interference and a rupture in our marriage. Although the relationship between Max and me was by now neither happy nor healthy, I could never have betrayed him.

The psychiatrist prescribed an assortment of sleeping pills and tranquillisers and assured me I was not going mad but suffering from an acute nervous anxiety.

After the visit Max asked me two direct questions. 'Did you tell him about the club in Edinburgh? Did you go into details about our sex life?' I replied in the negative to both enquiries and a look of relief appeared on his face.

I told him that I had filled in a questionnaire asking if there was any history of mental illness on either side of my family. I had said that I had never heard of any relative, alive or dead, who had suffered from any kind of mental disorder. (This was perfectly true.)

It was at this point that a very strange thing happened. Max turned very quiet, poured himself a large whisky and sat down beside me. In a low, subdued voice he told me that his one real fear in life was of going insane.

I was startled to hear him talk like this, for it was the first—and only—time he ever revealed any weakness. I tried to make a joke of it by saying it was me, not him, who seemed to have a 'screw loose' and that he had far too brilliant a mind ever to lose it, but for the first time in our married life I had seen fear on Max's face. That night he drank himself into a stupor and I slept a prescribed sleep.

Years later, when it was too late, I wondered if it should have been Max, not me, who went to see the psychiatrist that day.

The depression lasted for several months, but I eventually stopped taking both tranquillisers and sleeping pills. This was a mistake, for soon the tearful anxieties returned, accompanied by fits of shaking during which I couldn't even hold a newspaper steady enough to read the large print. I had heard that lots of people who suffered from nerves resorted to cigarette-smoking—so I smoked my first cigarette. I bought one packet, then another and another. I have smoked ever since.

All at once, in the spring of 1963, something happened to lift my spirits high. A sudden onset of sickness, I thought, was probably tummy nerves. I postponed going to the doctor. Then all the other symptoms of pregnancy appeared and our family doctor confirmed that I was expecting another child. Max was taken by surprise at first, then expressed his delight and hope that this time it would be a son to carry on the name Garvie.

A sixth sense told me I was going to give birth to a son. I just knew. I was deliriously happy, knowing that there was a new life inside me and more than certain that my pregnancy would leave me immune to Max's obsessions with nudity and unnatural sex.

I overestimated, and stretched my happiness too far. Max argued that my pregnant state shouldn't interfere with the holiday he had planned for us at a naturist place in Corsica.

We flew from Heathrow to Ajaccio that summer. I was three months pregnant. We arrived at 'Tropica', a private naturist reserve south of Bastia, in the early evening and were greeted by the proprietor, a middle aged German doctor named Klapperstuk who lived on the property with his wife and family.

For the next two weeks we lived in one of the many 'bungalows' scattered about the grounds. It was a cheaply-made construction of two small rooms with neither water nor sanitation. Water and toilets were fifty yards away. The place was sparsely-furnished, with the room shared by Louise and Claire also serving as kitchen and lounge. It afforded only essentials—double bunk beds, a table, chairs, a two-ringed gas cooker, pots, cutlery, crockery and a plastic bucket for carrying water from the tap.

Several hundred men, women and children of various European nationalities swarmed the colony, enjoying the 'freedom' of nudity. The situation in general seemed much healthier than in the awful cottage near Edinburgh and for the next fortnight I swam with the stream. It was considered in extremely bad taste to wear clothes at any time during the day, but it was perfectly acceptable to dress for evening and only people suitably attired were allowed to enter the bar, where you could enjoy a snack meal and drink local wines. Or the evening could be spent walking through the grounds, where the perfume of the flowers mingled with the pungent, bitter-sweet smell of the earth.

The beauty of Corsican sunsets fascinated me. They were like ripened peaches that seemed to burst and flood the sky with flame. Later, when darkness descended, the oil lamps of remote mountain dwellings could be seen twinkling in the distance, and along the coast the curved arms of the Mediterranean clasped clusters of village lights. Their sparkling reflections made them look at times as if they were stretching over to strike a light on the still, sleeping horizon.

Although I still hated the idea of nudism, the nature reserve in Corsica was easier to bear than my previous experiences.

A few months after we returned to West Cairnbeg—in December 1963—my son Robert was born. Max was delighted to have a son at last, but in my heart I knew that Max and I were growing further and further apart.

A few months after the birth, my ever-resourceful husband dropped yet another bombshell. The nudist club near Edinburgh, he said, was too far away and too inconveniently situated for regular use. He wanted to start up a club of his own. He had seen, he said, an advert in a local paper for a cottage near Alford, about twenty miles from Aberdeen. He thought this would provide an ideal base for his very own nudist club.

Max had mentioned several times before that he liked the idea of starting up a club, but I never really took any of these comments seriously. This time, however, he seemed determined. I was frightened, for I feared if the plan was realised there would be no escape either for me or the children.

Max went ahead and bought the place, which was later nicknamed 'Kinky Cottage' by the locals, and set about getting it ready for his purposes. It was a typical remote country cottage, much in need of repair. Max started to have it renovated and redecorated. He also bought hundreds of trees from a forester near Banchory which were planted round about to provide privacy and seclusion for the nudist enthusiasts he was certain would flock to join.

The opening ceremony was scheduled for a sunny, windy day in the early summer of 1964, and about twenty or so potential members turned up to watch the fun. I was told that I was to have the doubtful honour of performing the opening ceremony, and of course I was expected to do this in the nude.

This time I refused point blank. I felt the time had come to put my foot down once and for all. To Max's fury and disgust, his wife was the only one of the assembled company who was clothed. I cut the white tape dressed in a simple blouse and skirt, for by this time I couldn't have cared less how much he taunted me or how angry he was. The one thing I was certain about was that never, ever again would I appear before other people in the nude.

Tea, sandwiches and cakes were served and Max made a speech. I have no recollection of what he said that day to the faithful, and that was the very last time I had any connection with my husband's craze for the nudist cult. From that day on, whatever he did in his own club or any other he did by himself.

I was always anxious to encourage Max in any ploy which I thought might take his mind off nudism and demands for sex. In 1961 he had started learning to fly in order to get a private pilot's licence. He had always been a tearaway in cars and enjoyed the sensation of speed, so it was natural that the next step for a young man like Max with the means to do it was to take to the air. As with everything else he did, he did it well and within a few months the licence was his. In the months and years to follow I was glad that he spent so much time following his flying craze, for it seemed a much healthier pursuit than the other pleasures he enjoyed. In fact, Max began to lose interest in the nudist club after he took up flying. He rarely visited it after I had refused to have anything more to do with nudism, but on sunny Sundays he used to fly over the club for a low-flying peek at the nudists.

His aim, Max said, was to have his own private plane and to build a private airstrip and hangar on his farmland. He would start a new fashion by owning his very own aircraft and would become unique in farming circles.

After Max got his licence I flew with him occasionally, but it was a hair-raising experience and I never enjoyed it. He actually wanted *me* to learn how to fly and get a licence too and it annoyed him when I told him I would never have the courage to try! I was so scared during these flying trips that I got him to alter his Will to state that if we were both killed my mother would take care of the children. Max was a daredevil in the air and seemed to take delight in frightening his passengers. Like myself, they must have spent most of the flight with their hearts in their mouths.

Max's plans to build a landing area at West Cairnbeg were, however, foiled by the fact that the air currents in the area were wrong for the construction of an airstrip. The 'flying farmer' had to be content to rent a landing strip at Fordoun, about three miles from the farm. It was at Fordoun that he formed a flying club and 'parked' his own plane, a Bolkow.

But even his enthusiasm for high-flying speed thrills turned sour. It wasn't long before air stunts—to which he once treated our son Robert, aged four at the time—were losing their novelty. Max found that flying his plane only retained a thrill when he took to the air after consuming handfuls of Pro-Plus tablets washed down with large quantities of whisky.

He then started 'shooting up' cars on the Stonehaven road. The idea of this little game was to fly low towards a moving vehicle with the aim of terrifying both driver and passengers and of causing it to stop or slew off the road. Even his own family weren't immune to Max's new prank, which he thought, of course, was a tremendous joke. One day he recognised my car as I was driving back towards West Cairnbeg and swooped low towards me. I got a terrible fright and the car and I ended up in the ditch at the roadside. That was really amusing!

One day later in his flying career I took the children for a picnic to Stonehaven harbour, which was crowded that day with yachts and other craft. Suddenly Max's plane appeared and he swooped so low over the boats that people on board were terrified and I believe some of them ended up in the water. Max cleared the cliff-top on the other side of the harbour with only feet to spare. I was frightened and embarrassed and got the children together into the car and drove straight home. Max had been cautioned several times before about his flying stunts, but this time he was charged with dangerous flying. Again, it was all a huge joke and he said, laughing, that he would pay a QC to get him off.

He had got to the stage where he didn't know what to do

next for kicks—and he loved the feeling of power and being able to frighten people. I was afraid that he would kill either himself or someone else. I tried to reason with him, but it was like talking to a brick wall.

The next thrill he tried was politics. Max threw himself with great vigour into the Scottish Nationalist Party—and, of course, insisted that I join too, although I had no interest whatsoever in the SNP or any other party. His enthusiasm for the Scottish Nationalists took him on to the Stonehaven Committee of the party, and early in 1967 we went to an SNP rally in Stirling.

We were picked up by the bus in Laurencekirk, where we left the car, and off we went to the rally to listen to the main speaker, Winnie Ewing, and meet other Nationalist supporters. I felt like a fish out of water. On the way back we stopped at a little pub outside Perth for a few drinks, and Max bought whisky to drink on the bus on the way home. As the journey progressed, Max got drunker. He began to fool around, necking with me like a teenager. In the midst of all this we talked to a young man who had been at the meeting, a tall chap who told us his father had once run a hotel in St Cyrus.

The bus stopped in the deserted main street of Laurencekirk and I stepped off, carrying the remains of the day's packed lunch in a basket. From inside the bus, its engine still running, I could hear Max still fooling around and, to the annoyance of other passengers, refusing to leave his seat.

As I stood alone in the street, the young man we had been speaking to during the journey got off the bus and walked towards me. I suddenly got the impression that he felt sorry for me because my husband was making such an exhibition of himself. He smiled out of the darkness and said 'I'll walk you down the street to your car.' Taking the basket from my hand, he added 'Don't worry, he'll get off the bus!'

I had hardly noticed this lad, although I suppose you could say he was easy to spot because he had 'SNP' in large letters printed on his jacket! My own feelings towards him at that moment were of gratitude because what he did seemed like a nice, kind gesture.

Then the bus came down the street and Max stumbled on to the pavement. I drove him home, as Max was far too drunk to handle the car.

The young man stepped back on board the bus. His name was Brian Tevendale.

5

I had always though of marriage as sacred. The close-knit, conventional family atmosphere in which I had been brought up had instilled in me that marriage vows were for keeps, and although I was aware from the early days of my marriage to Max Garvie that all would not be sweetness and light, I never for one moment imagined that anything could happen to tear us apart. If, on the day I married Max, someone had even hinted at the tangled, twisted and bizarre series of events which led to the collapse of our life together—and to the final tragedy—I would have laughed outright.

In almost nine years of marriage Max, I knew, had never been with another woman. I had looked at other men—every woman does—but never in a thousand years would I have betrayed my husband or even considered being unfaithful.

A woman will do a lot for a man, and will endure a lot to hold her family together. I had gone along with Max's craze for nudism, which was completely alien to all my attitudes and beliefs, until I could take no more. I had suffered endless rows over his sexual demands, which to me were unnatural. I had watched many times the little plane taking off, knowing full well that, at the controls, Max was half crazy on a concoction of pep pills and whisky. I had hoped and prayed that a miracle would happen and things would get better.

The prayers fell on deaf ears. We were already caught in a downward spiral to destruction. The collapse of any marriage is sad. The collapse of mine was a nightmare of fear, degradation and twisted emotions which ended in the greatest tragedy of all.

The Max Garvie with whom I now lived was changing into a totally different person from the young farmer I had married nine years before. During the terrible days and nights which were to follow I often thought back to that day in Dunnottar Church in Stonehaven. My mother had wept as Max and I stood before the minister, and I became more and more convinced that she had experienced a real premonition of what was to come.

The young Max Garvie of those early years would spend many an hour poring over farming journals and magazines, engrossed in the agricultural life in which he was so talented. This new Max Garvie waited just as anxiously for packages from London to be delivered at the farm and would spend just as much time poring over their contents—pornographic magazines full of pictures of nude women, or women posing in kinky underwear or leather 'gear'. The young Max Garvie had happily taken holiday snapshots, pictures of us enjoying ourselves on our trips abroad. The new Max now wanted something different for his camera—to take photographs of his wife in the nude.

I was uneasy about the idea, but at least I would be appearing naked only in front of my husband. It was not like the Edinburgh nudist club. And, of course, the only person ever to see the results would be Max. Although I didn't enjoy posing for these photographs, I suppose in a sense I was trying to lose some of the inhibitions I was constantly being accused of having. Besides, there were no onlookers.

We had two photographic sessions, both in the sitting room at West Cairnbeg. Each time the children were safely tucked up in bed, and each time I had drunk quite a lot of alcohol so that I would feel more relaxed. Max used a Polaroid camera. My poses were seductive, but certainly not what I would consider pornographic, and he seemed delighted with the results. I was uneasy during these sessions, but I presumed the pictures would be put away safely in Max's wallet and would be for his eyes only.

Even in this I was wrong. One evening we were having a drink with a pilot who had flown up with Max to Fordoun from Biggin Hill. During the general conversation at the bar, this man turned to me with a smile and said secretively 'I've seen more of you than you think!'

At the time I hadn't the faintest idea what he was talking about, but his strange remark stuck in my mind and later, at home, I asked Max what he had meant by saying this to me. My husband said nothing, he simply laughed and pulled the nude pictures of me out of his wallet. I was shocked when I realised that my own husband had shown these photographs to a total stranger. As always, to Max it was just a joke. To me, it was a deep hurt and a betrayal of trust. That night we had a terrible row. How, I thought, could any man with any sense of decency be so cruel as to show nude pictures of his wife to another man? How could he be so unfeeling as to put her in a position where she was likely to find out that he'd done so?

There were no more picture-taking sessions at West Cairnbeg.

Max's interest in all the farming organisations and agricultural meetings at which he had been the leading light had been waning for some time and he no longer bothered with the social set in which we had once been firm fixtures. Instead, his money was buying him new friends with whom he drank regularly at his favourite watering-place, the Marine Hotel in Stonehaven.

He loved to be the centre of attraction there, surrounded by young men eager for a trip in the plane. Max was the big-time, wealthy farmer with the ever-open wallet, ordering round after round of drinks. He was hero-worshipped, for the big talk, the cash and the jokes never dried up. Max himself was drinking more heavily than ever—and so was I, in a futile attempt to blot out the days and nights of what was becoming an increasingly unhappy life.

Max was doing things which were totally out of character with the kind of life we had led before. One night, as we left a hotel in Laurencekirk, he started chatting to two young couples as we walked to our car. The two girls had obviously had a lot to drink and were very much 'under the weather'. But Max promptly invited this foursome back to the farm for a drink. We all piled into the car.

When we got home, Max supplied large drinks to every-one—and then suddenly went to bed, leaving me alone with four young strangers, with whom I had little in common and even less to talk about. I remember feeling angry and giving the two lads a good 'ticking off' for getting the girls so drunk. They eventually left.

As those months went by a worry began to creep into my mind—the worry that Max might start looking around for another woman. In all the years we had been married I had never had any cause to be suspicious of extra-marital adventures on his part, but there were signs that my fears could soon prove well-founded.

Max enjoyed the company of his young friends at the Marine Hotel a lot, but there was another group, an 'in' crowd he desperately wanted to join. It consisted mostly of couples around our own age. One night, as we talked at the bar, he told me we had been invited to a party at the home of one of these couples and we would be going along that night.

It was a beautiful house, there was a magnificent buffet spread and, as usual, the drink was flowing fast and furious. People swayed to the loud dance-music and everyone seemed to be having a good time.

Suddenly I found myself on my own. There was no sign of Max and I realised I hadn't seen him in the room for quite a while. Then I noticed that one of the women was also missing—so I decided to find my husband. I threaded my way through the company and asked someone if they'd seen him or knew where he was. All of a sudden, another woman moved in front of a door as if to bar my way. I pushed my way past into a bedroom, and there was Max with the woman, lying on a bed. He got up abruptly and pretended to be reading a newspaper. He was fully-clothed.

I was angry and, telling him I wanted to go home right away, left the bedroom to find my coat. He followed me out. We got into the car and started towards home, but a little way along the road he stopped the car, seized me by the throat and banged my head against the side window. I was crying and he kept shouting at me to stop, shouting again and again. He told me I had 'spoilt his fun'. This was the first time Max had ever been violent towards me.

For the next few days I wore polo-neck sweaters because I didn't want anyone to see the bruises on my throat.

I suffered in silence throughout all this, simply because there was really no-one I could talk to about the difficulties my marriage was going through, although they were getting worse and worse. Some women can endure a lot and I was one of those women. If I had been a weaker sort of person in that way, I might have decided to leave Max. I might have tried harder to find some source of advice which would give me the courage to abandon a marriage that was obviously going wrong. If I *had* walked out the subsequent events would never have taken place—but I didn't. I stayed.

The nights of drinking at the Marine Hotel continued as usual, and often we met the young man who had carried my basket up the main street in Laurencekirk that night when Max had refused to leave the bus. He was a pleasant, friendly, quiet sort of lad, Brian Tevendale, and Max seemed to get along well with him.

One night, Max invited Brian and another, older, man to go flying with him. They fixed a date for the flight the following Sunday. It was a beautiful, sunny day in April. Max went off to the airfield and I stayed at home with the children, basking in the sunshine in a deckchair in the garden. I didn't expect Max home for lunch that day, as he usually ate out on a Sunday, but suddenly the car rolled up to the farm and the three of them, Max, Brian and the older man, got out.

They were hungry, so I prepared some sandwiches and we sat around eating and chatting. I think I treated Brian in exactly the same way as anyone else who came to the farm. He certainly made no great impression on me—apart from the fact that he seemed a nice, ordinary sort of lad. That was the very first time Brian Tevendale visited West Cairnbeg.

One Saturday, not long after, Max announced that he was going to take me for dinner to Stonehaven's Bay Hotel— the scene of our small wedding reception twelve years before. I was pleased, for at least a visit to the Bay would provide a welcome change from our usual 'haunt', and I starved myself all day so I would enjoy my meal.

We began the evening with drinks in the hotel cocktail bar. Suddenly, Max announced that he wasn't hungry and that he wanted to go back to the Marine Hotel. We arrived in the familiar bar to find the familiar company, including Brian, crowded around it. Max was doing his usual 'big spender' act and the drinks really started to flow fast. Everyone knows the effect of too much alcohol on an empty stomach—I hadn't eaten a thing all day—and I got a little drunk. We were all fooling around and somehow—I have no idea how it happened—I found myself holding hands with Brian. Max noticed this perfectly innocent little incident and thought it hilarious.

Eventually hunger prevailed and four of us, Max, myself, Brian and one other man, left the hotel for a local fish and chip shop. I never got my promised dinner, of course.

As we drew near the shop, Max suggested I stay in the back of the car with Brian, but when he stopped the car Brian got out with Max and the other man. Some minutes later Brian came back on his own and told me that Max had sent him back to 'keep me happy'. We sat together in the back of the car. Nothing happened except perhaps just a kiss and a cuddle—we were both rather tipsy. I think Brian thought it was rather a strange thing for Max to have done.

Shortly afterwards the other two came back laden with fish and chips and we dropped Brian and the other man at their homes.

The following day I had a slight hangover and felt a little ashamed of having held hands with Brian and allowed him to cuddle me in the back of the car. Max simply laughed in his usual way and didn't seem to care.

By this time Max had become quite friendly with Brian. He started inviting him to the farm more and more often, and eventually Brian began to stay with us for weekends. Max had him doing all sorts of jobs around West Cairnbeg, including spraying the whole of the airstrip at Fordoun with weedkiller! When our hen man was away on holiday Brian, myself and the children would all collect the eggs. He and

Max seemed the best of friends, drinking together, joking together and fishing together in Stonehaven harbour. In the evenings at the farm the three of us would play records and have a few drinks. Then Brian would stay overnight in a spare bedroom.

All of a sudden, about this time, Max seemed to take a great dislike to bright lights. He removed the bulb from the light in our hall and replaced the ordinary white bulbs in the sitting-room lights with dark red ones. Finally he removed the elaborate central light-fitting from the ceiling of the sitting room and we were left with a large, gaping hole which was rather embarrassing when visitors arrived. There was never any point in arguing with Max. If he decided to do something, that was that. Nothing I could have said or done would have saved that lovely light-fitting.

He was still not content, for one night he put out *all* the lights and brought out candles I had used at Christmas parties. He said he preferred candlelight. Twice Max left Brian and me together in the room playing records by candlelight while he went to bed. On the third occasion all three of us had a few drinks—and then Max disappeared again, leaving Brian and me alone together in the darkened room listening to our favourite records. Brian asked me what I thought Max was up to. I said I had no idea. It did seem strange to both of us that a man should leave his wife in a romantic atmosphere with another man in his own home while he went off to bed.

That night, however, Max revealed at least part of what was going on in his mind.

When I went up to bed he started to ask me questions about Brian which I thought were revolting. He asked me to describe Brian in detail. Nothing had happened between myself and Brian Tevendale which would have made it possible for me to answer those intimate, sexual questions, even if I had wanted to.

I couldn't believe my ears, and I was shattered to realise that Max was under the impression that while he was upstairs in bed I was allowing Brian to make love to me. I was also frightened by this time, for I was now convinced that Max's attitudes towards sex were becoming completely sick and perverted. But worse, much worse, was still to come.

The day of the annual Fettercairn Agricultural Show dawned and off we went to attend. In previous years, this important local event had always taken us on to spend the evening at Edzell with the rest of the farming community. But this time, when the day's events came to a close, Max insisted that instead of staying with the local farmers we should head for the Marine Hotel. (Where else?) In the hotel bar he invited some of the regulars to come to the farm for drinks after we had been to a dance at Fettercairn.

There was no sign of Brian, so Max decided we should head for his home and persuade him to come along to the dance with us. When we got there we found Brian in bed and, naturally, he was not too keen to get up again. However, Max usually got what he wanted. Finally, he persuaded Brian to come with us to the dance and to the West Cairnbeg party afterwards.

When we arrived home there was music, dancing and plenty to drink, and one woman in particular got very drunk. It was getting late, so I went into the kitchen for some black coffee to try and sober her up a bit. While Brian and I were in the kitchen with her, Max stayed in the sitting room with her husband and another woman who had come with them.

After they had all left Max started making some rather odd remarks about what he had witnessed between this man and woman while he himself was pretending to be asleep. He seemed to have enjoyed being a *voyeur* and to get a curious sexual pleasure from watching the sexual activities of others. I was disgusted and tried not to listen to what he was saying.

A day or so later we were again back at the hotel in Stonehaven and met Brian, along with the regular crowd. After the usual rounds of drinks, Brian invited Max and me back to his home, where he lived with his mother. He told us that his sister, Trudy, her husband and their children were all staying there for the weekend and we would meet them too. Trudy's husband Fred was a policeman, and they lived in Aberdeen.

We walked into the lounge of Brian's home and there was Trudy Birse.

It was obvious from the moment he saw her that Max was attracted to this tall, slant-eyed woman with the boisterous, extrovert personality. He made no attempt to disguise the fact that he found her attractive. In fact, he immediately went over and sat beside her, oozing charm and quite openly 'chatting her up'. She made it equally obvious that she was reacting to Max in the same way, smiling seductively and gazing at him with those green, cat's eyes. I sat at the other side of the room and listened. Max invited her up for a trip in the plane, and they made a definite date for the very next day. I didn't know what to feel, as I don't suppose at the time I grasped exactly what was happening between them.

Twice that week Trudy telephoned Max at the farm and I listened in on the extension—to hear them arranging to see one another again very shortly!

A day or so later the storm broke. Max announced that he was going into Aberdeen to visit Trudy Birse.

I cried, I pleaded with him not to go—but Max's argument was simply that it was perfectly all right for people to do this sort of thing in the new permissive society. . . .

My feelings were not first and foremost of jealousy, but of a deep, deep hurt. All the love I had tried to give Max had been thrown back in my face, and everything I had endured throughout this strange and turbulent marriage meant nothing. I had tried so hard and I had put up with so much and Max didn't give a damn! For months I had feared, at the back of my mind, that Max would take a mistress—and now the worst had happened. Something was severed for good between Max Garvie and me the day he set off for Aberdeen to see that woman.

After he'd gone I stopped crying because there were no tears left. All that remained was a kind of coldness, an emptiness, a sense of loss—and the knowledge that the man I had lived with for all those years couldn't possibly love me. That knowledge was in itself a terrible thing; but what made it even worse was the fact that he was doing this so openly and making no attempt to conceal it from anyone, far less from me. Max had destroyed the sanctity of our marriage, something I had always tried to cherish, and he didn't care who knew about it! Although our sex-life had been impossible for me at times I had always regarded it as sanctified. Now he had made it seem cheap and horrible. All feelings of love, respect and loyalty towards him vanished that day.

I never felt any hatred for Trudy then or later. Indeed as the bizarre sequence of events progressed and I saw how he was using her, I felt sorry for her.

Max arrived back at the farm about 4.30 that afternoon, asked me casually how I was feeling and told me he was going back to see Trudy Birse again that same evening. He bathed, shaved and put on his best suit. He said he'd told Trudy that he was doing some business in Aberdeen and hadn't mentioned the fact that he was coming home before he saw her again. He then announced that he had arranged for Brian Tevendale to come and take me out that evening so that we could spend the time together while he was with Trudy.

At least I wasn't to be left alone. . . .

Max left, smart and spruce; and Brian arrived, young and—I felt—rather confused. We drove away from the farm in the Mark 10 Jaguar which Max had left us for the occasion and headed for the coast. We stopped at the St Cyrus Hotel, had a couple of drinks and talked for a while.

The day had been a nightmare, but now I had succeeded in relaxing a little and found this young man's company strangely comforting. I remember telling him something of what had been going on between myself and Max and found Brian very understanding. It was a tremendous relief to talk to an ordinary, down-to-earth young man with an ordinary job and ordinary interests. Here I could sit and talk about normal things—and forget for a while about Max's sexual obsessions, cars, drinking and flying.

Although it was obviously rather an odd situation—I was out for a drink with this young man while my husband was with his married sister—I think Brian and I felt very much at ease with one another that night. We spent a couple of hours together, then drove towards Fordoun. Max had arranged that we should rendezvous with him at the airstrip at 11 p.m.

We sat in the car near the hangar. There were a few kisses and cuddles, as I was much in need of comfort that evening, but nothing more. We sat, talked and waited. It was pitch dark and silent. Suddenly we both jumped as the car door was flung open and a powerful torch shone into our faces. Then I heard laughter—Max's laughter.

He must have driven up as quietly as possible, with his car lights switched off, hoping to catch us in a compromising situation. I'm sure he was disappointed, because I knew by now that he wanted to see something happening between Brian and me.

I remember he laughed for a long time.

6

I don't believe that this new Max Garvie—who was a completely different person from the man I had married—was now capable of experiencing any normal human emotions. He could easily manipulate people for his own twisted satisfaction, but his inability to understand emotion made it impossible—even for the all-powerful 'flying farmer' of the Mearns—to control the results of the chain reaction he was now setting off. During the turbulent events of the next eight months Max tried to control people like puppets. But the puppetmaster was playing with fire. He simply overlooked the fact that his 'toys' were actually real human beings in whom he was to spark off a blaze of all-consuming passion.

In the late summer of 1967 I was aware that Max saw a lot of Trudy Birse. Any passing hopes that I might have had that Max, having taken a mistress, might lessen his sexual demands upon me had proved futile. The demands actually increased, for Max told me openly that Trudy was performing sexual acts with him that I had never allowed. If Trudy could do these things, why couldn't I?

He suggested many times, moreover, that I have sexual intercourse with Brian.

One night in September the three of us, Max, myself and Brian, again sat drinking at West Cairnbeg. All evening Max had again been saying to me in private 'Why don't you go to bed with Brian?'

The bizarreness of this suggestion—that I should sleep with another man in our own home while my husband slept alone in our bed—was dulled by the effect of the drink I had consumed that evening.

Brian eventually went to bed, to the spare room he always slept in when he stayed at West Cairnbeg. Max continued to go on and on about me sleeping with Brian that night. I ignored him and went upstairs to our own bedroom. On my way back from the bathroom, I found Max standing in the corridor, obviously very excited. He more or less pushed me into Brian's room, told me to stay there and closed the door behind me.

I was not in a fit or stable emotional state to understand my motives fully when I first slept with Brian Tevendale. In some ways, I suppose, it was a relief to get away from Max. But looking back now I find it hard if not impossible to put into words my feelings at the time. There was of course the fact that Max had hurt me deeply the day he went to start his affair with Trudy Birse, and I think there was an undercurrent within me of feelings of revenge towards him. In a way, perhaps I wanted to get my own back on Max.

Whatever my motives, I slept with Brian that night and we made love which was tender, natural and normal. When dawn broke I got up and went through to our own room—to find my husband delighted by what had happened and sexually excited by the fact that I'd had intercourse with Brian. He insisted on immediate sex and seemed to get a tremendous kick out of it because I had just come from Brian's bed. I had lost every ounce of respect I had ever had for Max, and physically I felt nothing for him. From then on, every time we were intimate I felt as though I was being raped by a stranger.

For a long time I had felt myself growing closer to Brian Tevendale. I was clinging to him now because I felt he was protecting me from a husband who no longer acted like a normal human being. I was frightened of Max, and what was happening—between Max and Trudy, myself and Brian—was beyond my understanding. Brian had become the only person in the world on whom I could depend and who cared about what happened to me.

We were falling in love.

It is impossible for me now to say whether or not I would have fallen in love with Brian Tevendale under normal circumstances. I was only given the option of one set of circumstances—and they were far from normal. But there are many different kinds of loving and sometimes love grows from strange roots.

I felt a little like I had that day at Max's own nudist club when I had refused to undress. I simply didn't give a damn any more: my marriage was in ruins and I had, quite literally, been pushed into the arms of a young man who gave me love, comfort and protection from the insane existence which had formed around us. Max was a stanger to me, emotionally and physically, and the only man who mattered to me now was Brian.

But although these feelings for him were deep and real, at times it was as though I was looking on while another Sheila Garvie acted out the things she did during this period. It was like standing back and watching another 'self' performing these actions while the real, normal, ordinary Sheila Garvie looked on in horror. It was a defence mechanism which allowed me to cope with a bizarre situation.

The four of us spent nights together in hotels in Edinburgh and Glasgow. I can't even remember the names of these places. Max, as he had always done, made all the arrangements. Max slept with Trudy and I stayed with my lover, Brian, for by now I was in full agreement with all that happened. I no longer cared: I was just glad to be with Brian. Max enjoyed it all immensely and was excited and enthusiastic about the whole set-up.

My emotions were completely confused during this period of sexual entanglement. On the one hand I was deeply hurt that Max had finally cast aside our marriage; on the other I was feeling more and more love for Brian Tevendale.

There was, however, enough left of the normal me to be anxious about what the outside world thought of our conduct, and it was hard for me to meet the gazes of people in our immediate circle and those who lived near us. I was ashamed of my behaviour, and the last thing I wanted was to have anything to do with the neighbours. I tried as much as possible to keep to myself from day to day, avoiding close contact with people I knew well. Instead of shopping in local stores where I would be a subject for speculation, I preferred to go to shops in Aberdeen, where I could be just another anonymous housewife.

I knew very well that my mother had a good idea of what was going on between myself, Brian, Max and Trudy Birse, but I also knew she would never take me to task. It was she who looked after the children during this time, taking care of them both at West Cairnbeg and at her own home in Stonehaven.

I was sure in my own mind, too, that people in the Mearns had more than an inkling of what was going on, but I had no idea how much they knew. If even a hint of the complex sexual liaisons had reached their ears, however, I knew gossip would be rife in the farming community. I was very involved in the complexities of my own feelings at the time, but I was still sufficiently ashamed of my behaviour not to risk the additional pain which might be caused by a disapproving eye, or a veiled comment from someone I knew.

The ordinary Sheila who had grown up in a strict, decent family and who had tried to live a normal married life, however, had vanished. A new, strange Sheila had taken her place. Some of the things we did that autumn seem almost unbelievable to me now.

Sometimes, at the farmhouse, there were only the three of us—Max, myself and Brian. When this happened Max would suggest that he and Brian toss a coin—a penny—to see which of them would sleep with me. One night, when Max had lost the toss for the third time, he suggested that the three of us go to bed together. This excited him terribly, and I think he intended that both he and Brian would have sex with me. But in fact, although the three of us were in the same bed, nothing happened. I felt like an object being passed around from one to another. I lost all respect for myself and felt utterly degraded.

At the same time, Max was giving Brian money to entertain me, to buy clothes for himself and to take me out wining and dining in hotels.

When Trudy was able to stay overnight at the farmhouse a new procedure was evolved. Max and she would set their alarm for 5.00 or 5.30 a.m. and this was the signal for her to leave Max's bed and knock on the door of the room where Brian and I slept. I was then to leave Brian and go through to Max's room, while Trudy would go to another bedroom. When I got into bed with Max he expected me immediately to have intercourse with him. As I've said, it was like rape. . . .

Then came the night when yet another person—Trudy's policeman husband—was involved. Max told me that he and Brian had been talking in a Stonehaven pub one evening with Trudy's husband Fred, who had said how much he would like to come to a party at West Cairnbeg.

I don't know just how aware this man was of what was actually going on. Max said he and Brian had wondered how we could keep to the usual arrangements and how Max could sleep with Trudy if her husband was there. As far as Max was concerned, however, this was an additional thrill which he assumed would add spice to the proceedings. He talked excitedly about putting a sedative in Fred Birse's drink so that he would pass out and know nothing about what was happening.

Trudy and her husband duly arrived at the farm on the night set for the small 'party' and we all started the evening with a drive to a hotel in Edzell for drinks. By closing time it had been arranged—by Max, presumably—that a girl from the hotel was to accompany us all back to the farm. This girl, whom I had never seen before, was to provide company for Fred Birse.

The candles were lit, the music played and the drinks flowed as always. Eventually I went upstairs to bed with Brian. I learned from Max the next morning that Fred Birse had—very sensibly—merely driven the girl back to Edzell, although he had left Trudy to spend the night at the farm.

Obviously, a situation like this could not go on forever. The potful of emotions which Max had concocted was about to boil over. It began to dawn on him that the relationship between myself and Brian was no longer purely a sexual one and that we were deeply in love with one another.

There was a row. Max told me he had no feeling at all for Trudy Birse and that my relationship with Brian had to stop.

He couldn't have cared less who I slept with as long as I didn't become involved. I don't think he would even have minded me starting up a liaison with Trudy's husband!

There was a meeting at my parents' home in Stonehaven in November. My mother had an inkling of part of what had been happening, but my father knew nothing about it except that something was very wrong. The meeting was an attempt to patch up our ruined marriage. I spoke for some time with my father alone and told him about the demands which were being made on me. He promised he would speak to Max to try and ease the situation, but added that at all costs I must stay with my husband at the farm for the sake of the children. This continued to be the opinion of both my parents on the subject.

By this time my nerves were beginning to crack. All the tension, the confusion, the turmoil and the drinking of the previous months were beginning to tell and Max phoned our local doctor, who prescribed tranquillisers.

The next day Brian phoned Max at the farm and asked him for a meeting in Stonehaven. A few hours later Max called me to demand that I should drive into Stonehaven and meet him in one of the hotels.

I took my son with me—Robert was just four and I couldn't leave him—and drove into the town. Max, of course, had been drinking. He told me there and then that I had to choose that day between him and Brian—and if I chose Brian he would put a bullet between my eyes!

I told him I loved Brian and wanted to be with him. Max stormed out of the hotel, locked the car I had used to drive into Stonehaven and drove off in another car. Brian took me to his mother's home and the next day I went to consult a lawyer in Aberdeen about the possibility of getting a divorce. I outlined to him roughly the sort of thing that had been happening. He told me that divorce might prove difficult to obtain because I too had committed adultery. All he could advise was that I should 'take the children and go back to my mother'. My mother's attitude, of course, was that my place was at West Cairnbeg with Max.

I asked Brian to pick up the two girls from school that day

and in desperation headed for the Bay Hotel in Stonehaven. I stayed there that evening with the children, and then our local minister arrived to say that Max had asked him to come and talk to me and persuade me to return. Then the manager of the hotel took me into his office and tried himself to convince me of the effects a split between myself and Max could have on the children.

If my husband had been a postman or a farm labourer, everyone would have said 'Leave him! Get out!' But Max was a powerful man in the community, popular and with a great deal of influence, and everyone was on his side—the doctor, the minister, the hotel manager. My parents wanted me to go back and I had little or no help from the Aberdeen lawyer. I wasn't married to a postman or a farm labourer. I was married to the mighty Max Garvie—so therefore everything must be all right and I was just being a silly woman.

The minister spoke to Brian, who left the hotel about 11 p.m. that evening. After my talk with the hotel manager I gave in and asked him to phone Max, who was at the door within half an hour to take myself and the children home.

The next day my mother arrived at the farm to help out and to assist me in looking after the youngsters. I decided that I was prepared, despite all that had happened, to try and make a fresh start and attempt to rescue our marriage from the ruin it had become. I knew it was going to be difficult to forget Brian, as my feelings for him were still deep, but I was determined to try and get over my lover for the sake of my children and my marriage.

The few weeks before Christmas 1967 were uneasy, but bearable. Then, just before the festive season, shades of the past cast a gloom over my attempts at a reconciliation. Max told me that Trudy Birse had started leaving little notes on the windscreen of his car. Whether this triggered off something in Max or not I don't know, but he became restless again and started going back to meet his old friends in his old haunt, the Marine Hotel. He liked the company there, he said. Brian was there too. Why wouldn't I go with him? I refused to entertain the idea, and there were more rows between us.

It was a strange situation. Max had been furious when I had become emotionally involved with Brian Tevendale. I had promised and resolved to give him up and start afresh. And here was my husband trying to persuade me to go back to a place where he knew I would meet my former lover. Max could not—or would not—see the problem. He made light of the whole thing and couldn't see any reason why I shouldn't accompany him to his favourite bar. He was a regular there the whole of the month of January and we had quarrel after quarrel because I refused point blank to go with him.

In the middle of February I finally relented. For the sake of a little peace and quiet I agreed to go with Max to the Stonehaven hotel. I knew very well that Brian would be there, because Max kept telling me he was.

I had not seen Brian since the meeting in my parents' house in November. I had promised not to and I had kept my promise faithfully. A few days before I was due to pay this visit to the Marine Hotel, however, I telephoned Brian at his place of work in Aberdeen and met him in a cafe in the city. I told him what had been happening and how the rows and tension were beginning again. I warned him that I had agreed to go to the Marine with Max. I didn't want to cause any trouble.

On the Saturday night we paid our visit, and Brian was there as expected. Everthing, however, passed off smoothly—but the next day Max was told by a so-called well-meaning friend that Brian and I had been seen together in the cafe in Aberdeen. My husband was convinced by this that I had been seeing Brian secretly. That night he went on and on asking me repeatedly what had happened between us. I got to bed at four in the morning.

After that we went to the hotel several times—and then total confusion exploded over the whole scene again. On the one hand, Max was inciting some of his young admirers to throw Brian over the Stonehaven harbour wall. On the other, he was telling me that he would be delighted if I would be friendly with Brian once again. Not only that—he also suggested we start up another tangled set of relationships! He would like me to have sexual relations with another man, he told me, as long as I didn't get involved.

Then he switched back to the first issue—that my relationship with Brian should be renewed. He sent me to Brian's home to tell him that we both wanted to be friendly and that Max bore him no grudge about what had happened. I went. Brian told me he had been invited to a party in Stonehaven at the end of that week. Would we like to go? I told Max. He said we would definitely be at the party; no doubt about it.

We duly arrived at the house where the party was. At first Max and Brian seemed to get on quite well, just like old friends. Then Max suggested that Brian and I should dance cheek to cheek, taking a malicious delight in the reactions of the other guests when they saw this. It was very hurtful, for we both knew we still felt deeply for one another.

We drove Brian home that night and returned to the farm. Twenty-four hours later Max told me he wanted us to renew our relationships with Brian. He put on all the romantic records I associated with Brian. I was very upset. Max then went out drinking and I stayed at home alone.

I was now fully convinced that Max's mind had completely gone and that I could finally take no more of this life with him. I simply couldn't carry on. In an impulsive moment I later bitterly regretted I telephoned Brian and begged him to take me away. Fortunately, the children were staying with my mother that weekend.

I threw a few things into a small case and drove our estate car to Stonehaven to pick up Brian. We drove into Aberdeen, left the car at the station and stayed the night with a relative of Brian's. The next day he phoned Trudy and within a few hours she arrived. That was the first time I had seen the other member of our curious foursome since the day of the 'conference' at my parents' home in November.

Trudy drove us to Bradford, for she told us she had a friend there with whom we would be welcome to stay. Within days I found an office job, but in my heart I knew I had done the wrong thing. I could not bear to part with my children and I was missing them terribly already.

I had made a mistake. I should never have asked Brian to take me away. I had to get home to the children. The thought crossed my mind that perhaps even the children might not be safe with Max, knowing the way he was.

I phoned Max from the Bradford office. The first thing he said was 'Do you want to hear Robert crying?'

Max told me he would meet me at Heathrow Airport. I left Bradford without saying goodbye to Brian, headed for London and sent a telegram to him before Max arrived.

He had hired a taxi with the registration letters COW, and as we were driving to a hotel he just kept saying '*Cow, Cow, Cow!*' We stayed near London for one night, then Max hired a car to take us north.

It had originally been planned that we would go on holiday to Peebles in April. We were now into March, and it was decided that my brother should bring the children south and we would meet up in Peebles for an earlier holiday. I begged that we should stay there as a family for the holiday for the sake of our children, but Max refused and went back north to West Cairnbeg. He came back to collect us the following Sunday and drove us home. That same night he insisted I go—yet again—to the Marine Hotel for drinks with his friends.

I had no idea whether Brian had come back from Bradford or not and whether he would be there. He wasn't. I didn't know whether to be glad or sorry. I felt like an outcast amongst Max's friends as they laughed and drank.

A few days later Max started really hitting the bottle. He also began to ask me intimate questions about what had happened between myself and Brian in Bradford. That night I took six tranquillisers. I wanted to shut myself off from Max and this life of misery. Max telephoned the doctor late at night and told him I had taken fourteen of the pills, which was a lie.

I went into our dining room while he was on the phone and sat down. Max went upstairs. Ten minutes later he came back down and put on every light in the house. He smashed a glass against a radiator, picked up some of the broken pieces and held them inches away from my face. He hauled me from

72

the chair by my hair, took hold of my left arm and forced it up my back. I screamed and screamed because I thought he was going to break my shoulder. He shouted at me to call Brian a horrible name, but I refused. Then he threw me against the wall. I lay there for a while trying to blot out the pain, and eventually I crawled upstairs and lay down on a bed.

The next thing I remember was the doctor arriving the following day. He suggested I attend a psychiatric clinic.

I telephoned my mother. She arrived at the farm and bandaged my shoulder and arm with a crepe bandage, for the whole arm was badly swollen and very painful. She told me Max had told her that I had tried to commit suicide and I assured her—since she was very upset—that this was completely untrue.

I went to the clinic, as advised, and saw a psychiatrist there. I remember him telling me about the rows he had with his own wife and how he loved to watch girls walking up and down Aberdeen's Union Street in their mini skirts. What all that had to do with me I had no idea. Then Max was brought into the room and the psychiatrist said that if I wanted to kill myself there was nothing he could do to stop me. It was clearly pointless trying to tell him I had no intention of taking my own life.

During the next few days Max drank very heavily. One evening he came in roaring with laughter because some of the locals at the pub in Auchenblae had been asking him what kind of disinfectant I drank—presumably referring to the suicide attempt I was supposed to have made.

Things got worse and worse. Max taunted me night and day. He said I needed mental treatment and should perhaps be put into a clinic in London.

One day I went shopping in Stonehaven, and as I was putting groceries into the boot of the car, Brian came over to speak to me. It was purely a chance meeting and the first time I had seen him since I came back from Bradford. He asked me how things were and I told him. He said that a lot of men got rid of their wives by putting them in mental hospitals and that I was to be careful.

When I got back to the farm—a fairly short drive—I found that Max had already been told by yet another 'well-meaning' friend on the telephone that I had been seen talking to Brian.

April passed, then soon it was May, and life at West Cairnbeg went on much the same as before.

Some of the cast of a Royal Deeside pageant, including children
of members of the staff at Balmoral.
I acted the part of Queen Victoria.

Above: Family
Right: Wedding and Honeymoon

Opposite page: West Cairnbeg farm and farmhouse
Above: Max and myself in his plane

Max and Trudy Birse

31.—**North-Eastern Counties, Bucksburn** (Co.). Since 15th ult. from his home at West Cairnbeg, Fordoun. **Maxwell Robert Garvie**, b. (Laurencekirk) 24.10.32 (35 yrs.), farmer, 5ft. 10in. c. sallow (tanned with rough blotchy skin), deep forehead, h. bn., brown bushy eyebrows, e. blue, full lips (lower protrudes), broad chin, good teeth. Spends freely. Is a heavy spirit drinker and often consumes tranquilizers and " Pro-Plus " tablets when drinking. Is fond of female company but has strong homosexual tendencies and is often in company of young men. Wearing mid-brown s.b. 2-piece suit with faint dark red pin stripe and horn bone buttons,

white shirt with small checks, brown shoes, small badge in shape of pilot's wings in jacket buttonhole. May be wearing S.N.P. badge, wristlet watch with black strap. Has in his possession brown folding wallet containing cheque book issued by Clydesdale Bank Ltd., Auchenblae with Serial Nos. E2984176-200 ; Midland Bank Group Credit Card for £30. ; Membership card of Scottish Aero club ; driving licence and photographs ; thought to be in possession of considerable sum of money (may be almost £1,000) but this cannot be checked. Is a man of considerable wealth and until 3 or 4 years ago was completely rational. Of late he has become very impulsive, probably brought about by his addiction to drink, has threatened suicide on at least one occasion. Deals in pornographic material and is an active member of nudist camps and an enthusiastic flier and may visit flying clubs. May have gone abroad.

Among the 'missing persons' in the Police Gazette. . . .

Above: My lawyer Mr Laurence Dowdall, my Counsel
Mr Lionel Daiches QC and Mr Brian Hughes,
Mr Dowdall's partner, arriving for the trial
Top right: 'Queues and crush barriers'
Right: Lord Thomson inspecting the guard of honour

My mother

Queues and crush barriers . . then 100 hear
stories of
four in a
love tangle

● QUEUING UP . . . more than 200 people were turned away from the packed High Court in Aberdeen.

WIFE WEEPS IN MURDER COURT

Sheila Garvie's mother, Mrs. Edith Watson, is helped into an ambulance after she collapsed

Mother collapses as she is asked about marriage

THE mother of a woman accused
of murder collapsed while giving
evidence yesterday.

Mrs. Edith Watson, 59, swayed and fell only
seconds after she had taken the oath in a High
Court trial at Aberdeen.

She had been asked to recall
her daughter's marriage in
1955.

As she was led shouting
hysterically from the courtroom, her daughter, Mrs. Sheila
Garvie, 31, wept in the dock.

Mrs. Garvie, a slim attractive
blonde, is accused along with
two men, Brian Tevendale, 23,
and Alan Peters, 20, of murder-
ing her wealthy farmer husband
Maxwell Garvie.

They all deny the charges.

Emotion

Mrs. Watson's collapse at the
end of a day of allegations
about the love-lives of Garvie
and his wife produced the first
sign of emotion Mrs. Garvie
had shown all day.

She had sat stony-faced as
the court heard the dead man's
sister and a minister answer
questions about what went on
in "Kinky Cottage," a local
name for Mr. Garvie's "private
hideout room."

Defence counsel Mr. Lionel
Daiches, Q.C., also spoke of
farmhouse "foursomes" made
up of Tevendale and Mrs.
Garvie and Maxwell Garvie
and Tevendale's wife Mrs.
Trudi Birse.

The minister, the Rev.
Kenneth Thomson, told he
had been told that Garvie
invited Tevendale to seduce
his wife.

He said Mrs. Garvie had
complained to him about her
sex perversions her husband

made her take part in and of
physical ill-treatment.

Earlier, Mr. Ewan Stewart,
the Solicitor General, quoted
long passages from the Scottish
Police Gazette describing
Maxwell Garvie.

It suggested that he was a
free spender, a heavy spirit
drinker, fond of female company, but with strong homosexual tendencies, and often
seen in the company of young
men.

Barriers

That he took pep pills and
tranquillisers while consuming
drink dealt in pornographic
material, including photographs, this threatened suicide
and was an active member of
nudist camps.

The judge, Lord Thomson,
adjourned the trial until
today after Mrs. Watson's
collapse.

She was taken from court
to hospital and returned later
when treatment had enabled
her to resume her evidence.

Before this it was alleged Garvie
had carried a double-barrelled
shotgun around in a parcel
and said suicide bid involving
his gas.

Who
killed
Maxwell Garvie ■

FULL TRIAL REPORT
PAGES 5, 6 and 7

BUMPS-A-DAISY GOES THE QE2   PICTURE SPECIAL CENTRE PAGES

. . . and the newspaper story

Fred and Trudy Birse leaving the court after the verdict

Leaving Stonehaven Sheriff Court

Above: Gateside Prison
Top right: Cornton Vale Prison
Right and overleaf: My mother's letter

Given to Sheila to open by J. Mackintosh
1/6
on A/gr Instruction
24/5/49

Mrs Sheila Garvie,

Only to be opened by Sheila
if anything should happen to me.
from Mum

My Dearest Sheila,

If you ever receive this I will
be with my Mum & Dad. Don't ever grieve
for me myself that if you all still in Yateville
I will not be until the tears & that thought
is terrible to me, however you cannot bargain
with God, if I could, I would gladly give up my
life to be able to let you free. Don't ever
give up, keep your head high, you will never had,
never, as always remember that if I can I will
be looking after you from somewhere so that if me
standing beside you always. It was, if we had
known the saddest part of your life when you
married into the Goldric, no wonder I cried at
the time you were being married. You have
always been greatly loved by me & the love
I that for you has never changed, although
perhaps at one time you thought no. I

cannot write now my heart is too full of having
to leave you & the tears so please let
God Bless you & may you be happy yet
so I think you will. All my love forever
until we meet again.

Your most loving
Mother.

Sheila

I think I was only given
about this time by the Dr's
in Aberdeen so all the usual
happenings had actually nothing to do
with my illness.

Mum

7

The morning of Tuesday 14 May 1968 dawned cloudless, sunny and warm. Louise and Claire went off to school, and a little later Max left West Cairnbeg to visit his father.

It was a perfect day, a day to spend outside in the warm fresh air, and my little son Robert and I spent most of it moving marigold seedlings from the greenhouse and planting them in the garden. I remember enjoying that day. Despite the unhappiness and confusion of my existence it was still possible to sample with pleasure the simple things of living, like a day in the garden in May with my little boy.

Just before tea-time, and before the girls' arrival home from school, I took a long, cool shower and felt reasonably relaxed. It had been a pleasant day, and I have always loved the sun.

Max arrived home. He had arranged to take a girlfriend of my brother's for a flight in his plane that evening, but about six o'clock he took a telephone call from my brother saying that the girl wouldn't be going after all. I don't know the reason for this change of plan: perhaps the girl hadn't turned up, perhaps she and my brother had decided to do something else, perhaps she had simply got cold feet about flying. While Max was talking on the phone I overheard him saying also that he thought he might go to an SNP meeting in Stonehaven that evening and if he did he would probably see my brother in the Marine Hotel after the meeting was over.

I never knew quite what Max was going to end up doing, for his movements were so unpredictable. He was always changing his plans from one moment to the next. The previous evening had been a fine night, clear, bright and perfect for flying and Max had decided to take the plane up for a spin. He got all dressed up in his flying gear then at the very last moment, for no apparent reason, he suddenly decided not to go. His mind flipped so quickly from one idea or plan to the next it was well-nigh impossible to be certain that he would actually do what he had planned.

The other man in my life, Brian, I had seen only three times since the disastrous trip to Bradford. I had met him on that one occasion in the street in Stonehaven and I had telephoned him twice when I was in Aberdeen and arranged to meet him in a shopping arcade in Union Street. There I had told Brian what had happened to me in the days after our chance meeting in Stonehaven. He said that if I ever decided to leave Max again he would take me away. I was torn in two, for although I knew I still loved Brian I also knew that I could never, ever, leave my children; and I told him that. I had last seen Brian the previous week.

On that fateful Tuesday evening, Max left the house in his own Cortina not long after he had spoken to my brother on the phone. The farm garage was now empty, for my car was being repaired in Laurencekirk and Max's Jaguar was in Aberdeen. He had smashed it up by running off the road into a field after a night's drinking.

When Max left I was sitting working at my knitting machine, the girls were out in the farm grounds with their pony and little Robert was playing just outside the door.

I had no idea whether Max would come home alone, or perhaps with my brother. A week or so previously Max had been tipped off that the local police could no longer overlook his drunk driving. They were becoming concerned about it and Max's informant had warned him to watch his step. I suspected that my brother might come back to the farm with Max that night because Max would be worried about driving himself home.

The children didn't come inside until about 8.30, for it was a lovely evening and I didn't mind them making the best of it and enjoying the late sunshine. I made them supper as usual and got Robert off to bed. He slept in the same room as the two girls, a bedroom just a couple of yards along the landing from our own. As always, I lay down beside him and read him some of his favourite stories until he finally fell asleep.

Downstairs in the sitting room Louise and Claire were by now glued to the television set, and I went down to join them. We talked a little as we watched and the two of them—Louise was twelve and Claire eleven—pleaded with me to be allowed to watch their favourite programme *The Avengers* which didn't start until 10.30. Although they had a portable TV in their own bedroom, they usually came downstairs and sat with me while Max was out, rather than leave me sitting alone.

We watched about twenty minutes of *The Avengers*, then I decided it was time for them both to be in bed. I assumed that Max would be drinking somewhere—probably the Marine Hotel as usual—that evening and I always wanted the children to be in bed before he got home. The reason for this was quite simple. . . . I never knew what state Max would be in when he arrived home late and it was best, I thought, to have the youngsters safely upstairs, so that they would never have to witness their drunken father making a scene.

I didn't want to disappoint them and deprive them of watching the last half hour or so of their favourite TV programme so I told them that if they were very quiet and switched on the portable TV in their bedroom very low, they could watch the rest of it upstairs. 'But please' I asked 'don't waken your little brother!'

Some time after 11 p.m. I crept upstairs and peeked into the room to find them both sound asleep with the TV still on. Quietly I switched it off, put out the light and closed the door.

Max arrived back around 11.15, about ten minutes before the programme ended. He was alone and had obviously been drinking. I asked him if he had seen my brother, but he said no. The meeting—in another hotel—had been late in finishing and there hadn't been time to get to the Marine Hotel to meet him.

As usual, he poured himself a drink and asked me if I wanted one too. I had a gin and orange. As we sat with our drinks Max started talking about his 'anti-sex' pills, as he called them. He took Soneryls—pretty powerful sleeping pills which doctors have since discovered are addictive—and told me that he had phoned the local doctor the previous day to get more of them.

I was shocked at this information. The week before the doctor had come to the farm to see how I was and I had taken the chance to tell him that Max was now bragging about drinking five bottles of whisky a week and taking the pills as well. I told the doctor about his habit of downing handfuls of Pro-Plus tablets along with whisky, and then going up in the plane. The doctor had promised he would try and have a talk with Max about all this, as obviously mixtures of whisky and various types of pill couldn't be doing him any good. I therefore asked Max now if the doctor had not suggested he go and see him, rather than simply prescribing pills over the telephone, but Max said he hadn't. He'd been told he could just go along and collect them at the chemist.

We went on talking and then Max got around to his favourite topic of conversation—sex. By this time whenever the word was mentioned my whole body froze. The talk turned into another of those interminable rows we were always having on the subject.

I went through to the kitchen and took a bottle of Soneryls from the cupboard. I took two of them. I remember being angry about them being there at all. There were still pills in the bottle. Here was Max phoning the doctor for more, before the ones he had were even finished! I went to the toilet downstairs, then climbed up to bed at about midnight. I can't remember the exact time.

No-one had called at the house that evening and the only telephone link we'd had with the outside world was my brother's call at around six. The doors of the farmhouse were unlocked as always, for it never occurred to us to lock up at night. Most country people were the same, at least in those days.

I didn't fall asleep right away, for Max followed me upstairs almost immediately, undressed, got into bed and we had sex. Because of my lack of physical feeling towards him by this time, I could never describe it as 'making love'. It was purely sex. After this interlude I got out of bed to wash my hands at the basin in the bedroom, then I lay down beside my husband and fell asleep. I don't recall how long it was before I slept, but it must have been well after midnight.

As usual I had left our bedroom door open and the light on the landing on. I always did this in case the children woke for some reason—I would then hear if they were awake. The light on the landing was left on because my son would often wake and come through and slip into bed beside me.

Now all was quiet at West Cairnbeg. It was a still, windless night and every living thing inside the farmhouse and round about it slept peacefully.

How long I was asleep I have no idea. The next thing I remember was someone tugging at my arm. My first thought was that it was one of the children. But as I struggled through that dream-like state between sleeping and waking and managed to focus my eyes a bit I saw a tall figure, much taller than any of the children, beside the bed. I recognised the voice of Brian Tevendale whispering urgently to me to get up.

I slid from the bed, my mind still woolly from the effect of the sleeping pills and Brian took my arm and hurried me out of the room. The light in the bedroom was still off, but the landing light was on, as I have said, and I caught a glimpse of a fair-haired lad—a stranger—standing just outside the door near the curtain at the end of the landing.

Brian took me along to the bathroom, thrust me inside and told me to stay there. I noticed suddenly that he was carrying a gun, its barrel pointing downwards towards the floor. I had no idea what time it was and my drugged brain couldn't cope with the problem of what Brian was doing there with this other lad. I was confused, dazed and bewildered. I stayed, as I was told, in the bathroom. A door closed. Then I heard terrible thumping noises. That's the only way I have ever been able to describe them, thumping noises.

It only seemed like minutes later that someone was trying the door of the bathroom, which I must have locked although

79

I don't remember doing so. Brian asked me to open the door, which I did. He said something to me—something like 'He won't worry you any longer. . . .' Then he told me to go and hold on to the children's bedroom door to make sure they didn't come out. The door of their room was only a couple of yards away from the door of our own bedroom.

My most vivid recollection of that night is of kneeling outside the children's bedroom gripping the door-handle with all my strength. I was only wearing a short white nylon nightdress and Brian came over and put something around my shoulders.

It had crossed my mind that the two had been giving Max a good hiding, because Brian had said once or twice that he deserved a good beating-up for some of the things he had done to me. But gradually it began to dawn on me that something far more terrible must have happened, although it never occurred to me that Max had been shot.

It emerged at the trial that the shots that killed Max were fired through a pillow. Police ballistics experts had carried out experiments at West Cairnbeg to find out what you would hear in the bathroom if a gun was fired through thick cotton wool. Their conclusion—thumping noises. I was not aware that what I had heard were shots.

I have no idea how long I hung on to that doorknob, but as I knelt there on the floor I could hear noises and movements in the bedroom. Then I heard Brian and the other lad—whom, as I said, I had never seen before—going up and down the stairs. Eventually I knew that something was being dragged out of the bedroom, something long and heavy wrapped in what looked like a groundsheet. I looked round and saw it. Then I heard them pulling and bumping it down the stairs.

I knew then that Max was dead.

Brian came back upstairs and led me down to the sitting room. I asked him how he thought they would get away with what they had done. He replied that they would bury Max miles away and that if I said anything to anyone about what had happened I would be implicated and would spend twenty-five years in prison. I remember him also telling me to put the gun back in its place. I don't remember doing so; all I can remember is staring at the gun lying on the floor of the sitting room later on.

They left me sitting there, alone, in a chair in the sitting room. I heard a car start up and go away into the night. I had no idea what had happened to the thing they had bumped down the stairs. But I had asked Brian before he left if Max had suffered and he said no.

Now I was completely alone. I sat in the chair in my dressing gown. *I was alone.* Max was no longer there—he was dead. The children were asleep in their room, but our room was empty.

Max would never come back, not ever.

I just sat in that chair for what seemed like eternity. Every nerve in my body had knotted and twisted itself in fear and shock. I sat motionless, aching with terror and the horror of what had happened. Death had come in the night, had done its work and had left behind three innocent children and a woman—or what was left of a woman—immobilised by a shock so great she couldn't move a limb. My mind, like my body, was frozen in disbelief at what had happened that night at West Cairnbeg—at *West Cairnbeg*, which had been my home for almost thirteen years.

I sat in that chair, alone, all the rest of the night and slowly the beginnings of thoughts started to creep into the shreds of my mind. Guilt was the first. It came, searing through my brain like a red-hot knife.

I had had no knowledge of what was going to happen at the farm that night and I had no hand in the killing of Max Garvie, but I knew I was morally responsible for the awful deed. I had allowed Brian Tevendale to fall in love with me and thus become emotionally involved with me. I had unconsciously provoked him into committing murder because I had aroused in him a state of uncontrollable emotion. Under the influence of that emotion, Brian had done this dreadful thing. The longer I thought about it, the more guilty I felt. I blamed myself entirely, and I still do.

Brian had done this thing because of me! As the hours crept by and I still sat there I made a decision—to protect

Brian Tevendale with every ounce of strength and power of reasoning I had left.

I cannot recall what feelings—if any—I had for Max Garvie that night.

The telephone rang. The sound was like a sharp scream of agony tearing through my brain. The total silence that death had left in its wake was broken, and at last I had to move. My shaking hand lifted the receiver and I heard the bleep of a coin-box at the other end of the line. The voice that followed was Brian's. It seemed as though he was talking from a million miles away. Vaguely, I heard him saying that he had left the parcel in the garage and that I was to take 'them' in to Trudy's house and she would know what to do with 'them'.

As he talked I looked through the curtains and saw that it was already light. The world outside must be coming to life. Soon it would be time for the children to get up, and I had to get them off to school somehow. I would have to attempt to act normally and to go through the motions of this new day as though nothing had happened in the farmhouse that night. I didn't know how I would do it, but I had to try. I had made the decision to protect the man who had killed my husband and I had to try and make myself function like an ordinary human being beginning an ordinary day.

I ran through to the garage. It was empty of cars but there was indeed a parcel lying there. I lifted it and saw through the open end that it contained Max's suit. I took the parcel upstairs to our bedroom and put it in the back of the wardrobe.

That was the first time I had been in that room since I had been pulled out of bed, and as I swung round the sight of the mattress struck me with horror. It was covered in blood—Max's blood—and the blankets were all tumbled up in a heap at the bottom of the bed. I felt a wave of nausea break over me, but I managed to pull some of my clothes off the chair where I had left them the night before. I walked quickly from the room, my head spinning, and went downstairs to put on my clothes in the sitting room.

Only yards away from that awful room the children were still sleeping.

But it would soon be time for them to get up and go to school. How would I get them there? The garage was empty; there was no car to take them. The cleaning woman, also, was due to arrive about 8 a.m. Would I be in a fit state to speak to her?

The world was wakening up. Outside the farmhouse there were postmen about delivering letters, people getting up to go to work, friends who might telephone. There were farm workers already tending the animals, and business contacts of Max's who would want to know where he was and how they could get in touch with him. There were relatives who might come in on an unexpected visit. Inside that tiny part of the world called West Cairnbeg were a bloodstained mattress, an empty garage, a man's suit wrapped in a parcel and a terrified woman with a dreadful secret she had to guard from everyone.

Max Garvie had been murdered and he would never come back. The blood on the mattress was his and the suit in the parcel was one the 'flying farmer' would never wear again. Somehow the world must be prevented from finding out.

I didn't know how Max had been killed and I had no idea where his body had been buried. What I did know was that the truth must be concealed. Early that morning I began a course of lies and deception which was to last for three months. I told the children their father had had to go early to a meeting in Edinburgh, which was why his car wasn't there. I think I asked my older girl to telephone friends at a neighbouring farm to ask them if they would take herself and Claire to school. They may have come to the door to collect the girls, or the girls may have walked down the road to meet them, I can't remember. I have no recollection, either, of giving instructions to the cleaning woman that morning when she arrived, although apparently I told her not to go into the bedrooms.

I do remember phoning the garage in Laurencekirk to ask if my car was ready. It was, and they agreed to deliver it to the farm. When it arrived I drove my son Robert into Stonehaven and left him with my mother. Then I went on to

Trudy Birse's house in Aberdeen, but I had forgotten to take the parcel with me. I can remember being in Trudy's house some time during the morning of Wednesday 15 May but I have no idea what I said to her. All I do recall is that it was very trivial. Nothing was said about what had happened the night before. I had only been in the house a few minutes when her husband and another of her brothers arrived, and I got up and left.

I had taken quite a number of tranquillisers already that day to try and dull the turmoil in my mind, so many of my memories are vague and confused.

I returned to Stonehaven to collect the children, and took them back to West Cairnbeg. On the way I noticed Max's blue Cortina, the car he had taken to the SNP meeting the night before, parked at the airstrip, on the left-hand side of the hangar. I had no idea how it had got there.

Finally that evening, I got the children to bed.

I knew that the bloodstained mattress was still in the empty bedroom and late that night I phoned Trudy in a state of panic. She kept talking to me and telling me to get a grip on myself—and I learned later that that phone call lasted more than half an hour. I spoke to Trudy about the mattress, the mattress covered in Max's blood, and she said she would arrange to have it taken away and replaced with another one. I talked and talked: I didn't care what I talked about as long as I spoke to someone because I was almost at breaking point.

When the phone call was over I sat in that chair in the sitting room. Alone, all night, again.

The next morning, Thursday, I got the children to school somehow, then went to my mother's. She knew—I had told her the previous day—that Max was not at the farm and she said she would come back with me that day to help look after the children until he returned. We collected the girls from school and, at my mother's suggestion, spoke to the farm grieve and told him Max hadn't come back.

That evening my mother and I sat in the sitting room of West Cairnbeg together, talking. The conversation we had is rather vague in my memory, but I remember that I decided to tell her my secret—in a way in which she would assume that I had been actually involved, for I knew if I told her the truth about Brian and the murder she would have gone straight to the police. And I had vowed to protect Brian at all costs.

'I hope he won't come back!' she said.

I had to tell her; I had to tell someone! I couldn't bear the burden of that terrible secret all by myself and I trusted my mother with all my heart and soul. Up to that point I had told myself that I would take the secret of what had happened with me to my grave. I assumed my mother would do the same.

I told her 'Mum, he won't ever come back.'

Her face paled and suddenly she understood.

'You don't mean he is dead, do you?'

I said nothing: I just nodded my head.

'Did he suffer?' she asked, her voice reduced to a whisper.

'No,' I replied. That was all I could say about it, for that was all Brian had told me.

8

When I made that decision in the early hours of the morning after Max was killed, the decision to follow a course of deception to protect Brian Tevendale, I had no idea how much I would come to hate and despise myself.

Ninety-four days and ninety-four endless nights elapsed between the murder and the day of my arrest. The days were a constant round of deception and every hour of every day was filled with the fear that suspicion might attach itself to me. I was inching my way along a tightrope. One slip and Max's murder would be discovered—and Brian would be doomed. I felt like a snowball, rolling down a steep slope. While a snowball gathers pure white snow around it, however, I was gathering guilt and self-hatred.

The darkness of each night brought with it a reflection of the deeper darkness of that awful night in May. I spent hours tossing and turning in sleepless torment. When sleep did come it was the shallow sleep of pure exhaustion. Sometimes, when morning came and I lay in that blissful half-dream state between sleeping and waking, for a few short seconds my mind was calm and forgetful of all that had happened. Then it came flooding back into my brain, an avalanche of horror, and I knew I would have to face another day on the knife-edge. One false step could mean disaster.

I used to watch planes flying overhead and wish fervently that Max was in one of them. I wished to God that it had never happened. As time went on I hated myself more and more.

That Thursday, when I told my mother Max would never come back, she stayed the night at West Cairnbeg. At least

I was not entirely alone with my guilty secret. Mother now knew Max was dead and believed, as I had intended she should, that I'd had something to do with what had happened. I hoped this would ensure her silence. She went off to bed, but I remained sitting, fully clothed, in the same chair in the sitting room for the third night running.

It was well after midnight when the telephone rang. The voice at the other end was that of Trudy Birse. She and Brian were ready to come to the farm. Was it 'all clear'?

They arrived a short time later. From the back of Trudy's car they produced a brand new mattress, which they carried upstairs into that bedroom. They rolled up the bloodstained mattress and carried it downstairs. I don't recall helping them. My arm and shoulder were still stiff and sore from the night Max had twisted my arm up behind my back.

I gave them the parcel containing Max's clothing. It was put in the car along with the mattress on which my husband had died. In the early hours of the morning Brian and Trudy drove away—I assumed they went back to Aberdeen.

Upstairs, my mother and children were sleeping, but I went on sitting in that chair for the rest of the night.

My next worry was the car—Max's Cortina, which was still parked beside the hangar at the Fordoun airstrip. The following day, a Friday, I drove with my mother to Aberdeen to ask my brother if he would try and find keys to fit the car, as I was anxious to get it back to the farm. I had no idea what had happened to the originals. My brother found a selection of keys, but none of them were any good and the Cortina had to stay where it was. On the Saturday I remember going to the home of the chairman of the flying club, and during our conversation I asked him if he could help in any way to find keys to fit the car. He was very kind and said he would do his best to come up with a suitable set. If he did he would take them to the airfield the following day.

Then it was Sunday, the fifth day after the murder, and I went into Aberdeen—to telephone Brian from a kiosk and ask him to meet me. I was desperate to see him; to talk to him. There had been little or no communication between us since the night Max died. As we drove along, I asked Brian who the other lad was, the young man who had been with him that night. He told me his name was Alan Peters and he had met him at work. Alan had been going out with a girl called Helen who had become pregnant and the two of them were hoping to get married as soon as possible. He assured me that Alan would never breathe a word to anyone about the murder because he had taken just as big a part in it as he, Brian, had done. I wasn't to worry about him 'talking'.

I had decided I must never betray Brian, but if my plan of deception succeeded would I always be strong enough to bury a secret like that in my mind for the rest of my life? Would some day the pressure become too great and would I be the one to crack? There were so many lies to tell. The next step, I knew, was to report Max's disappearance to the police.

I had become numbed to all feeling, and it was as though everything else I did, all my elaborate attempts to deceive, were part of a role in someone else's tragedy. I had never been a liar or a deceitful person, and I hated everything I did. It was against all my natural instincts.

That same day, the Sunday, I telephoned Sergeant Robert Grant at Laurencekirk Police Station and told him that Max had gone missing. I added, however, that I was certain he would turn up at an important flying club meeting which was due to take place the following evening. I told the Sergeant that I would check to see if Max did turn up at the meeting— as I was sure he would—and that if he didn't I would phone the police station again.

I went through all the right motions. I phoned the meeting and asked if Max Garvie was there. I was told he wasn't—of course—so later that evening I again telephoned Sergeant Grant to inform him that Max had not in fact turned up as I had hoped and that I now wanted officially to report my husband missing.

Ironically, Sergeant Grant was the same police officer to whom Max had reported *me* missing in March when I left to go to Bradford with Brian Tevendale.

The next day was Tuesday, a week after Max's last night

alive, and Sergeant Grant came to West Cairnbeg. He arranged to have me call at the police station that afternoon. By the time I got there, I was shaking with nerves, my stomach knotted with tension. Outwardly I suppose I must have appeared to perfection the worried farmer's wife wondering where on earth her husband was and what he was up to.

Sergeant Grant was a kind and sympathetic man and I remember the shame and revulsion I felt at the time for having to tell him all these lies. I said that Max had come home from the SNP meeting the previous Tuesday evening and had immediately started drinking. We'd had an argument about sex and I had taken two sleeping tablets and gone to bed. I had wakened, I said, the following morning just before seven to find Max hadn't been to bed at all. I searched the house, but there was no sign of him. The garage was empty. His car was gone. I said I hadn't thought much about Max's disappearance at the time as he had been due to take the plane to Strathallan for servicing that day and from there to travel to a meeting at an agricultural college near Edinburgh.

I told the sergeant I'd seen Max's car parked next to the hangar at the airfield the day he vanished—and I'd assumed he had gone off in the plane. But when I had checked the hangar on the Thursday the aircraft was still there. Then I thought that perhaps he had met up with someone else and they'd travelled direct to Edinburgh in a different car, leaving the servicing of the plane for another day.

Every word of this was, of course, a lie, all part of the course of deception on which I was now set. I was trapped like a fly in a spider's web, a web of shame. I couldn't cut myself free and there was no turning back. The lies would have to go on and on.

Sergeant Grant came back with me to the farm that day to look at Max's guns. Fred Birse had instructed me on how to remove fingerprints from a gun. Wipe it with an oily cloth, he had said, and this I had done. There was therefore nothing to be learned from any of the guns. I think the police thought it likely that Max had killed himself. Little did they know he really was dead, but not by his own hand.

Max had now been officially reported missing and the story about the disappearance of the 'flying farmer' of the Mearns hit the local and national newspapers. The police had asked me for a picture of Max and his smiling face appeared alongside stories about his sudden, mysterious disappearance. I didn't know this at the time, but Max's description had also been circulated in all copies of the *Police Gazette*.

I began to sense that the detectives investigating Max's disappearance were growing suspicious about the complete lack of clues as to his whereabouts. No longer was I only protecting Brian, I felt, but myself as well. Brian, I should add, had already been interviewed by the police during the search for the missing man and had contributed information about Max's homosexual advances to him which had been mentioned in the *Police Gazette*.

Brian had hinted to me that Max had made odd advances towards him. I myself had thought it strange that Max should want to associate so much with young men. And I will never forget a night he told me he loved Brian. However, I never knew anything much about homosexuality, or even understood its implications. It was a closed book to me at that time: I was very naïve about that aspect of life.

Max was now, like hundreds of others on police files all over the country, classified as a 'missing person'. The buzz of speculation among the public and the press continued for a while—longer than in most cases of its kind—but then, as in every other case, interest in the whereabouts of the missing man gradually waned. I cut myself off from the world as much as I could during those three months. I did my shopping in Aberdeen and if, on occasions, I bumped into someone I knew who asked me where I thought Max was I simply said 'I don't know.'

There were six people in the whole world who knew for certain that Max Garvie was not 'missing', but dead. They were myself, Brian, Alan Peters, my mother, and Trudy and Fred Birse. As I grew to hate myself more and more I also grew to feel more and more under the 'spell' of three of those people, Brian and the Birses. Trudy and Brian were very close and she was very protective towards him. She had a very domineering personality. I almost felt, in her company, that I was at her mercy. And when her husband and she were together, to me it was almost as though they were actually thriving on the situation. Something terrible had happened in which they were involved, but terrible though it was it had added a macabre spice to their dull life.

Trudy Birse never showed any sign of sadness over what had happened to her former lover. For this reason, when she later gave evidence in Aberdeen High Court, I couldn't understand her tears in the witness box. She enjoyed being in control of the situation: it was almost as though she was revelling in it.

My relationship with Brian was different. I was still in love with him and wanted to be with him as much as possible, but he didn't understand how I felt—how miserable and ashamed I was of being involved in this tangle of deceit. There was a hardness about Brian which, in a strange sort of way, was a help to me. When he shrugged off what had happened almost casually it seemed to calm me down. But this hardness blunted his appreciation of my own feelings and fears. I was the wife of the missing man. It was me who had to answer all the questions, deceive all these people— not him, nor Trudy, nor Fred. They had none of this burden to bear.

I still loved Brian and we still made love. It was true that I was making love with the man who had killed my husband, but I believed that Brian had committed the crime for me because of all the things Max had done to me. It seemed to me that Max had created a many-headed monster of twisted emotions around himself and part of that monster—Brian— had hated him enough to destroy him. Brian didn't appreciate, however, the day-to-day horror of the life I was now being forced to live. I needed him to cling to—there was no-one else—but he couldn't understand why I cried so much when we were together.

Before Max was killed I had loved Brian deeply. He had been an island of love and comfort in a sea of insanity. Now, however, I could detect feelings of resentment growing within me towards him for being the cause of all this chaos and misery and for depriving my three children of their father. Our love was not and could never be the same. What possible chance of happiness could there ever be for two people living under the dark shadow of a murder?

On many nights we made love, but I knew in my heart that people like Brian and me, bound together though we were by a dreadful secret, could never grow any closer in love. Gradually resentment, bitterness and the weight of that secret would destroy the love that had been and tear us apart. I never for one single moment imagined that I would ever be happy again. But I had made the decision not to betray Brian—there was no-one else, I thought, to protect him—and I had to abide by it now.

Brian and Trudy had taken away the bloodstained mattress and the parcel containing Max's clothes. But two weeks after the murder I noticed to my horror that there were still signs in the bedroom of what had taken place that night. To start with, there were bloodstains on the carpet. I hadn't noticed them before because they had not shown up clearly against the pattern. I scrubbed and cleaned the dark patches as best I could. Then I looked at the walls. Max's blood had stained parts of the wallpaper near the bed. Again, I tried to wash away the stains, but to make sure no traces would show I moved around the bedroom furniture, including the two heavy wardrobes, to cover them up.

Never once during all this did I think of what might happen to me if the truth was revealed. I simply lived out my shameful deception from day to day. It was abhorrent, but it wasn't very difficult. In the latter days of my marriage, after all, I had endured a very abnormal life with a very 'sick' husband and I was used to putting up a front.

At no time did I judge it safe to sit and collect my thoughts. I was trapped and there was no alternative open to me. But I do remember, one day, sitting in a café in Aberdeen, screaming and screaming inside to have this awful burden taken away from me somehow.

During those ninety-four days only two sets of visitors, as far as I can remember, came to West Cairnbeg. One of the visits was from the minister and his wife; the other was from Max's insurance agent. I knew nothing about Max's insurance policies—except that they always required very detailed discussion because of his mania for dare-devil flying. Nor did I know the contents of Max's Will.

I gave the family solicitor instructions for the administration of Max's estate on the assumption that he was genuinely missing. This made yet another person I was deceiving. I also made out a Will of my own on behalf of the three children. I had decided that if I was unable to summon the strength I needed to keep this awful secret permanently I would take my own life. I was aware that the day might come when I simply could not endure living any longer with the knowledge of what had happened. I asked my mother to get me a bottle of tranquillisers which I kept close by me in case the pressure became too great and I made the final decision to end my misery. Even in this I was torn in two. Although they didn't know it, the children had lost their father. What would it do to them if they lost their mother as well?

On 26 July Alan Peters was married to his fiancée, Helen. I had already seen him at the Birses' house and had recognised the young man who had been with Brian at West Cairnbeg that night. I never had much communication with Alan, but I learned that his intended bride was living in a caravan with him, and that she was ill.

Two or three weeks before the wedding Brian told me I was to be a witness, as he had been asked to be best man. I told him I didn't like the idea as I didn't want to be involved— but of course I already was.

Alan's fiancée's mother, who lived in Fort Augustus, was under the impression that her daughter was living in Trudy Birse's house, and once or twice I went with Brian to deliver her mother's letters to the caravan. I learned eventually that the girl—who was only six years older than my elder daughter—was suffering from a kidney complaint. I felt sorry for her. On one occasion I even took a prescription for her to an Aberdeen chemist and brought her back the pills.

On the day of the wedding I asked Alan Peters to carry his bride-to-be up the steps of the registry office because she had such a sore back she could hardly walk. He didn't, so it was me who helped her. I got a chair from the registrar for her as soon as we got inside.

I deceived many people during those months but I will never admit to looking after Helen because I was afraid Alan Peters would 'talk'. I quite simply felt sorry for her. It would have been difficult not to.

The little reception in the Birses' home afterwards was the most bizarre gathering I have ever attended. Of the six present—myself, Brian, Trudy, her husband, Helen and Alan Peters—only the bride was unaware of the truth about the murder of Max Garvie. Helen's presence, however, meant we had to think of other things to talk about. Brian had told me to bring along some food and drink because, he said, Trudy had enough on her hands getting the house ready. I took a small turkey, some tomatoes from the farm greenhouse and a cheap bottle of wine. I also gave the couple £5.

I should say at this point that although five of us knew Max was dead, I for one never knew how he had died. I never asked Brian for details, because I didn't want to know. I could not have coped with the knowledge.

Brian was working by now in an Aberdeen pub. The proprietor, who knew I was friendly with Brian, asked me if I would be willing to help out in the evenings during the Glasgow Fair Holiday (the second fortnight in July) as seven of his staff had walked out on him. Trudy, who wanted the money, got a job there too.

My mother was staying at the farm with the children and for the first few nights—I worked from eight till ten—I drove myself home. After that I changed to going back to Trudy's house in Aberdeen with Brian and leaving for home in the early hours of the morning. Never once during those three months did I spend a whole night away from the farm, although it was always terrible to go back there.

My mother hated Brian and wanted me to give up my relationship with him. If it hadn't been for her, he would have come to the farm. He wanted to be at the farm, although I don't know why. One night in August I telephoned my mother to tell her that the car wasn't going properly and I couldn't drive Brian home as planned. He had offered to drive me back to West Cairnbeg. My mother was furious. She didn't want him near the farm or the children.

On the morning of Friday 16 August my mother and I had a last, terrible row over my relationship with Brian. She then left the farmhouse. I assumed she would go home to Stonehaven and probably telephone me later. Just after midday I was preparing lunch for the children, my own three and the local minister's two little boys whom I was looking after for the day. There was a loud knock on the door. I opened it to see three detectives standing outside. I showed them into the sitting room and they told me that my mother had gone to the police to make certain allegations in connection with my husband's disappearance and they wanted me to go with them to Laurencekirk Police Station.

I asked them if I could take a coat with me and lifted a raincoat from a hook on the wall. My mind was whirling. I told my elder girl to watch the potatoes, which were just about ready to be poured, and one of the detectives told me that the wife of one of the farm workers had been asked to look after the children until my mother returned. The detectives then went into Max's office and took the guns.

I stepped into the police car, and the driver started the engine. As the farmhouse of West Cairnbeg faded into the distance I wasn't to know then that I would never see my home again.

9

The shock of my arrest was deepened by the knowledge that my mother had betrayed me. My mother, whom I had loved and trusted all my life and to whom I had confided my darkest secret, had gone to the police and told them Max had been murdered. As the police car sped over the long, narrow roads of the Mearns I sat in silence, thinking of that night in May when I had told my mother at least part of the truth. I knew my mother hated Brian and wanted me to stop seeing him, but I never imagined her hatred for him was strong enough to make her betray the daughter who had trusted her—and whom she believed to be involved in the killing. I had deliberately allowed her to think that I had been involved in order to protect Brian. It seemed now that I had made a mistake.

We had indeed had angry words that morning, my mother and I, but I thought she had merely gone home to Stonehaven. I never dreamed that she would go to the police at Laurencekirk and blurt out hysterically the confused story which had sent them into action.

My mind was in a turmoil as, after half an hour at Laurencekirk Police Station, I was taken to Headquarters at Bucksburn, on the outskirts of Aberdeen. The next thing I remember clearly is sitting on a little wooden chair in a small room. Detectives took turns to question me. I have no idea how many there were; they were just different set of eyes, mouths, voices and teeth. The questions went on and on—always the same questions: differently phrased, but the same.

My answers, too, were the same. They worked very

hard to break me down but. . . . No, I did not murder my husband. . . . No, I did not know where he was. . . .

Outside the day slowly slithered into darkness and they switched on a bright light in the room. A detective brought me a cup of tea and a biscuit, then stood over me, motionless, staring fixedly at me as I bit off a piece of biscuit and managed, painfully, to swallow it. My mouth was parched, so I tried to sip some of the tea, but his eyes never wavered, nor did he move from my side. The only sound in the room was the clattering of the cup on the saucer, for my hands were shaking badly. Finally I gave up, for I could neither eat nor drink, and I put the uneaten biscuit and the full cup of tea back on the table in front of me. The questioning began again. Sometimes the voices were soft and toneless, sometimes harsh, sometimes loud and vehement. Then an unbearable silence would follow. The hours dragged by endlessly. Midnight came and I was told suddenly that Brian Tevendale, who had been arrested about six o'clock that evening, wanted to see me.

I was taken downstairs into the room in which they had been questioning him. I was bewildered, for I couldn't understand why they were allowing us to talk together. I was even more surprised when all the detectives left the room and left us alone to talk without police supervision.

Later I learned the reason. The room had been 'bugged'. It turned out, however, that the equipment hadn't worked properly.

Brian had been desperate to see me, he said. He would have assassinated President Kennedy if only they allowed him to see me! We talked about the methods they had used to question us and the different detectives who had conducted the endless sessions. Brian told me he had met a detective who had known his father—who had been in the police at one time. I told Brian how upset and panic-stricken I was about the children. Who was looking after them? What had they been told? Were they all right?

Then came the next, staggering shock. Brian started talking about a woman in Banffshire who had accidentally shot her husband and got off with it. If she could get away

97

with it, surely I could too? He wanted me to admit that I had killed Max accidentally.

I was outraged by his plea. I had spent three nightmare months covering up for him and deceiving everyone into thinking Max had simply vanished, and now the man I had protected was betraying his cowardice by wanting me to take the blame for something I didn't do. I refused to agree to what he suggested.

I was taken back to my room. The night wore on. Then I was told Brian wanted to see me again. We had the same sort of conversation as before. It lasted for about half an hour. This time, however, I think they brought us some tea.

We never discussed what we were going to say to the police. I think it later became obvious that we had not concocted any joint story. I had decided to carry on with the same deception and the same attitude I had been taking for the past three months. I imagined that Brian would do the same and would stick to his story that he hadn't seen Max for months and had no idea where he was.

The night dragged slowly by. At last daylight crept into the room, softening the harsh glare of the light above my head. Then came the next shock. Early in the morning I heard activity outside the room and the muted murmur of voices. A detective came abruptly into the room and told me they had found the body of my husband.

How could this be? The only person available who could supply information to the police as to the body's whereabouts was Brian. Had he confessed? If so, what had he told the police to make them keep me in custody? He must have decided to reveal where he had hidden Max's body soon after his second conversation with me.

A thousand questions whirled around my mind. Where had they found the body? Had Brian taken them to it? What were his motives? Why had he given away the closely-guarded secret we had lived with for three months?

I have no idea what time it was when they told me Max's body had been found. All I know is that it was daylight and I had managed to eat some of the breakfast they had given me.

That morning, Saturday, I was charged with the murder

of my husband at Bucksburn Police Station, and a little later Brian and I were driven to Stonehaven to appear before the Sheriff. I remember little of the journey and don't remember having any conversation with Brian at all.

I think the Sheriff was rather taken aback when we appeared, for I believe it was the first murder charge to be read out in the little court buildings for seventy years. The solicitor who appeared with me in the Sheriff's Chambers had already told me that the Aberdeen firm he worked for really only dealt with property and similar matters, but he assured me he would get someone properly qualified to represent me.

After our appearance before the Stonehaven Sheriff I was taken back to Bucksburn where I was fingerprinted and had my picture taken several times. Then I made my decision. I had been charged with murder. I had very little idea of what was going on. I had been separated from my children and was tortured with worry about them. The world had finally collapsed.

It was time, I decided, to tell the truth at last.

The days, the nights of deception were over and I was going to tell the police exactly what had happened that night. I asked to see the Inspector and made a full statement of what had happened during the night of 14 May at West Cairnbeg farmhouse.

I told him everything, how I was wakened from my bed, removed to the bathroom and how I heard the terrible noises I will never forget. I told him how the body had been dragged down the stairs and how Brian and the other lad, Alan, had taken it away. I had been questioned for thirty-three hours, virtually non-stop, and I was so tired I couldn't remember Alan's last name. At that point my weary brain gave up. When the last line of the statement was read back to me my mind just wouldn't work any more.

I made that statement late on the Saturday afternoon. At eight o'clock the same evening I was taken to Craiginches Prison to spend my first night behind bars.

Yet another part of the endless nightmare was over. The next was about to begin. Fortunately for me the crushing weight of mental and physical exhaustion dulled the horror of my first night in prison. I had been crying for hours, my face was swollen and my head was splitting. I was allowed a hot bath that evening and I remember how difficult it was to stay awake as I lay in the water. My limbs felt like lead and my puffy eyelids drooped with exhaustion. I was so totally exhausted that for the only time in almost ten years in jail I was not conscious that night of the heavy door grinding shut and the metallic screech of the big key turning in the lock.

It was a big cell. There was one bed, a chair, a table and a small wardrobe. The walls were black, and my only contact with the outside world was a narrow, barred window high up in the wall. I awoke early the next morning, Sunday 18 August, to spend my first long, lonely day behind prison walls. The prison governor came to see me that day, but he didn't stay long and I can't remember much about his visit or anything at all of what he said to me.

At eleven o'clock that night a doctor was called to my cell. I was in a terrible state and torn apart with worries about the children. I was given a sleeping pill and tranquillisers to calm me down.

I couldn't sleep and I couldn't eat. Within days my body seemed to shrink to half its size and I was given a special food to counteract weight loss. Every time I drank it I vomited it up again.

Every Sunday I was weighed. To do this they had to take me to the doctor's surgery in the male section of the prison. I vividly remember the smell, the stale, acrid smell of sweat and urine, the sour smell of people who have been locked up together for a long time.

The two lights in my cell burned harshly day and night and I was under a twenty-four-hour watch. I was allowed books to read. I tried to make use of them, but after a few short sentences they were laid aside. It was impossible to concentrate. Knitting needles were out. I requested to be allowed to knit as I thought that might help to relax me a little, but was told on no account would that be possible. I presume they thought I might attempt suicide.

A woman prison officer had been brought up from

Gateside Prison in Greenock. She escorted me from my cell to the toilet. My meals were brought into my cell and mostly taken away again uneaten. I was completely isolated from the world. One day I asked if it would be possible for me to change the bed around in the other direction so that the constantly burning lights wouldn't be glaring directly in my eyes as I tried to sleep. The request was granted.

I remember one prison official who came to see me from time to time. She was kind and gentle and talked in a soft, comforting voice. We used to sit for a while on those days drinking tea she had made. She was the only bright spot on the horizon and I looked forward to her visits. I can't remember that woman's name now, but I will always be grateful to her for her kindness.

After two months, the prison officer from Greenock was replaced by another woman who allowed me out of my cell to do some scrubbing and polishing. One day I got a bucket of water and some cleaning paste and set about cleaning my own cell. When I started scrubbing the walls I found to my amazement that their natural colour was not in fact black, but a pale green. I scrubbed the whole cell. The black colour was caused by years and years and layers and layers of filth. I don't think the prison governor was too pleased when he found out that my scrubbing and cleaning had uncovered years of neglect!

On a good day I was allowed out for exercise in the prison yard for half an hour, escorted always by two prison officers.

During the hours I lay sleepless I thought about my mother and my children. Bitterness towards her was building up in me, not so much because of what she had put me through but because she had separated me from my children. I felt I could never forgive her. She had betrayed my trust and taken me away from the three children, and during those three months in Craiginches Prison I hated her.

I exchanged letters with Brian, however. Mine were mostly general chit-chat about life in prison. All the letters were copied and sent to the police investigating the case. I remember one curious letter Brian sent to me, likening himself to the Four Horsemen of the Apocalypse. He said he was Conquest—because he had won me over from Max. He was Slaughter—he had killed Max. He was Death—he had left Max's body to rot in an underground tunnel. And he was Famine—because of the years he might have to spend without me.

I tore up all his letters. I had no idea at the time what happened to the ones I sent to him, but later I learned he had considered selling them to a Sunday newspaper.

I had been told by my solicitor that he had engaged a Glasgow lawyer for me, a Mr Laurence Dowdall, who was making arrangements to visit me. He was, I was told, a well-known criminal lawyer and 'the best'. I had never heard of him, for I had never bothered much about reading about criminal cases in the newspapers. It was a side of life which—ironically, perhaps—had never appealed to me. One prison officer at Craiginches, however, told me 'If I was ever in trouble, Mr Dowdall is the man I would choose to help me.'

The day Mr Dowdall was due to make his first visit to the prison the women's wing seemed to get an extra clean and polish. It was a very old building. I believe that since I was there a new wing has been built to accommodate women on remand.

Despite the prison officer's assurances, I was uncertain about meeting this stranger from Glasgow and hesitant about confiding in him. But he breezed into the room in which the visit was to take place, introduced himself, shook my hand, tossed his briefcase on the table and waved me to a chair, saying 'Sit down, my dear!' The room seemed to come alive in his presence and I sat down and looked into his warm, friendly eyes. He was a man in his early sixties with spectacles he kept taking off and putting on again. He had fresh features and his eyes creased into a smile as he stretched across the table and patted my hands, which were clenched together tightly. As I tried to control my shaking he asked me in a quiet, firm voice to 'tell him about all the trouble'.

Before he left the prison that day he told me he would come and see me again after he knew more about the case.

He saw me several times during the three months while

my defence was being prepared and I always felt a little stronger after talking to this man with the warm, friendly personality who always did his best to raise my spirits and give me hope. On his third visit he told me he had interviewed detectives working on the case. He produced the three statements made by myself, Brian Tevendale, and Alan Peters—who had been arrested on Sunday 18 August, my first day in jail.

Mr Dowdall pointed out that the three statements were unique in his experience. They were totally irreconcilable. Brian had said I'd shot Max accidentally and asked him to get rid of the body. Alan Peters's statement had related how I had let the two of them, himself and Brian, into the house, had given them a drink and put them in an upstairs bedroom until Max was asleep. I told Mr Dowdall immediately that they were both totally untrue and that in particular Alan Peters's statement that I had let them in to West Cairnbeg was an obvious lie as there was no lock on the door from the garage and I would not have needed to let them in.

The statement I had finally given to the police that Saturday afternoon, I said, was exactly how it had happened.

One day, another three men arrived with him to see me. I was introduced to Mr Lionel Daiches, the QC who was to lead my defence. He was most distinguished-looking with beautiful, silvery hair groomed to perfection, and I thought he would appear more at home on a film set than in a courtroom. He was charming, but I sensed immediately that he lacked Mr Dowdall's warmth of personality and kindness.

I also met the two other lawyers who were putting together my defence, the Honourable Mr Robert Younger and Mr Brian Gill.

They all spent several hours with me, going over aspects of the case and carefully concentrating on every detail of what had happened all those months before and after the murder.

After the gruelling interviews, they left, and I wasn't to see any of them again until the morning the trial began.

I sat in Craiginches in my cell and the date of my court debut drew closer and closer. For the first time in my life I knew the kind of loneliness that is not easy to describe. It was a feeling of being pulled down by a dark and murky whirlpool, stripped of self respect; alone in a silent darkness and separated from a world grown alien.

I became anxious for the date set for the trial to come. I had been locked up day after day for so long. At least the trial was something to set my mind upon, something to break the monotony and isolation of those solitary days of misery and anxiety.

I knew it would be an ordeal. I had never been in a court before and had no idea what really went on there. I would be fighting for years of my life. Yes, it would be an ordeal. Just what an ordeal I was still to find out.

When I was taken from West Cairnbeg I had been wearing a skirt, a blouse and an old raincoat. I had to apply to the Procurator Fiscal to get permission for my mother, who was still at West Cairnbeg, to send me a pale blue suit, the suit I wore throughout the ten days of the trial.

Then I discovered that already the excitement was building up in the columns of the newspapers. This was to be no ordinary trial—everyone was to be subjected to the biggest blaze of publicity and sensationalism to surround a Scottish court before or since. I was just merchandise for many. In private, the market price was soaring for pictures of me taken at dinner dances and weddings. I was deeply hurt that people I had thought were friends could do such a thing.

I was wakened in my cell at Craiginches Prison at six o'clock on the morning of Tuesday 19 November 1968.

I got up and dressed. I felt lost in that pale blue suit, because by the day the trial was to begin my weight had dropped to under seven stone. I was then given some tranquillisers. I was driven to Aberdeen High Court and entered the building from the rear along with my two co-accused. We waited below for a few minutes, and then the three of us climbed the sixteen steps from the cell area through the trap door into the dock.

The policewoman looking after me had been given instructions to let me take more tranquillisers during lunch breaks. The pills in the morning would keep me calm for the first few hours, the ones at lunchtime would help me through the afternoon and steady my nerves until I was taken back to Craiginches at the end of each day. I was fairly heavily sedated, in fact, throughout the trial.

It may have been the tranquillisers, but very little of those ten days in court seemed real to me at all. Once again, as I had in the days of the 'foursome', I felt like an onlooker, this time watching Sheila Garvie sitting in the dock listening to all the evidence. The trial passed for me like nightmare, a horrible dream that fades from the conscious mind when you wake, leaving only the memory of a few details.

There is only a small selection of events in that dream I can now remember with any clarity. I had no idea of what was going on 'behind the scenes', or how my defence was being handled. The legal battle that was being fought on my behalf was in the hands of my lawyers, and I myself had little or no idea of their plan of campaign as the procession of witnesses passed through the court.

My defence lawyer, Mr Laurence Dowdall, explains in detail the legal complexities of the trial in the postscript to this book. He is far better qualified to do so than I, for I'm afraid the accused woman in the Garvie case had very little idea of what was going on around her during those ten terrible days.

The first confirmation that this was indeed to be a sensational trial came when my lawyers gave notice that I intended to attack my dead husband's character 'in respect of his unnatural and perverted practices'. As on all of the nine days to follow the high-ceilinged courtroom was packed with press and public. There was a flutter of eager expectation as they prepared for really shocking revelations.

The procession of Crown witnesses began. The first real shock for me was the appearance of my mother in court that first afternoon. The strain proved too much for her. She was only in the witness box for a matter of seconds before she had to be helped from the court and into an ambulance. She was a tragic and sad figure, and she had only done what she felt was right. She wanted to protect the children, and the guilty secret she had kept for three months was too heavy to bear.

The next day she was able to give her evidence in full. She was in that witness box for two and a half hours and every second of it was agony for me too. I didn't think she could stand the pressure. She looked so frail and weary, I wanted to run and put my arms about her. I wanted to tell her of my forgiveness.

I listened as she told the court that she had decided she had to put Brian into the hands of the police, and to achieve that she had to involve me. She knew of all the things that had happened leading up to the night of the murder and I felt her agony as she was bound by the court to tell of Max's perversions and how he had changed her daughter from a normal, happy wife and mother into the member of a sex 'foursome' whose exploits had shocked the whole community.

My heart wept for her as I heard this decent woman—to whom mention of sex had always been taboo—explain in front of all these people how Max had told her that he and Brian had tossed a coin to see which of them would sleep with me. I felt her shame. It was all so alien to her, all so terrible. She looked so helpless. I realised then that I loved her as much as I'd always done, and she loved me.

Brian and I exchanged a few words in the dock, but I remember little about what was said. One word, however, that came from his lips I shall never forget. As my mother appeared to give her evidence, Brian whispered 'Judas!' He didn't appear to have any compassion at all, and cared little for how I felt.

Every day as I was driven to court I saw the crowds of people queuing up with their flasks and packages of sandwiches, waiting, watching. I'll never forget those rows and rows of expectant faces. Seats on the press benches were in such demand that representatives of those newspapers lucky enough to get a space were issued with special passes. One day I saw the newspapers. I was appalled. It was as though nothing else was happening in the world except the Garvie murder trial. Pages and pages were devoted to detailed evidence and there were pictures of everyone involved, the detectives, the lawyers, my mother, the Birses.

We had arrived at Trudy Birse's evidence by now. I vividly recall her telling the court how much she had loved Max. It would have been nearer the truth had she told the jury that while encouraging him in his sexual perversions she was also casting her green eyes over my role as his wife and mistress of West Cairnbeg!

I was shocked and horrified when she told the court that I had said to her 'It had to be done, I couldn't take it any more. There was no other way.' I had never said anything of the kind.

Then came her most damning accusation. She alleged—although she had not told my lawyers this—that Brian had told her I had let him and Alan Peters into the house and showed them to an upstairs bedroom until Max was asleep. And she maintained that he had said that *in my presence*.

I was completely taken aback. I have never entirely understood, to this day, why she said these things.

I had been more than hopeful that justice would be done in that courtroom during those ten days, but as the Crown evidence started to pile up against me I began to lose heart. Alan Peters gave his evidence. His story was confused, I thought, and I was amazed when he said he had seen two cars in the garage at the farmhouse that night—a blue Cortina (Max's car) and a white Cortina (mine). It was proved without any doubt that my car was in a garage in Laurencekirk that evening and I didn't get it back until the next morning.

Peters's defence lawyers were clever, however. The appearance of his young, pregnant wife in the witness box telling the court that Alan would never 'stand up to a fight' engendered a lot of sympathy, as did the appraisal of his character by his former headmaster.

On the third day of the trial, Crown Production No 14 was produced in court. It was an innocent looking cardboard box. But inside it was the yellowing skull of my dead husband, the most macabre piece of evidence to go before the jury. As the medical expert prepared to lift the gruesome exhibit from the box to point out the bullet wounds, Mr Dowdall leaned over to me and said 'Don't look!' He told me what was about to happen. I lowered my head and began to feel sick. I was allowed to leave the courtroom and remain at the bottom of those sixteen steps leading up to the dock until the doctor had given his evidence. I know the appearance of Max's skull in court caused a sensation. But, mercifully, I never saw it.

I was in the witness box myself three days running, for a total of nine hours. I was examined by my own defence counsel, Mr Daiches, then cross-examined. As I told Mr Daiches my story I remember the judge telling me again and again to 'speak up', as no-one could hear me.

Then I came under fire from Dr R R Taylor, counsel for Alan Peters, who seemed to me to be obsessed by finding out exactly when and where I had first kissed or cuddled Brian Tevendale. This part of his cross-examination seemed to go on for hours. I simply couldn't understand what he was trying to prove. He was so sarcastic!

When it came to the turn of Ewan Stewart, the Solicitor General, I was amazed to find that he hadn't done all his research properly. During his cross-examination of me he asked me about my work in a lawyer's office in Stonehaven. I had never at any time worked in a lawyer's office in Stonehaven—but my sister had! Somehow, he had got me mixed up with my sister. I was very surprised that such an eminent man as the Solicitor General could make such a mistake. Perhaps that is why it has remained in my mind when so much of what happened has vanished.

As all the cross-examinations drew to an end, my mouth and throat were swollen and parched. It was painful to try and form even simple words or short answers to the questions.

Alan Peters and myself had now given our evidence. Then a rather bewildered young man from Laurencekirk was called to give evidence. He was a joiner. He told the court how he had fitted a lock to the door leading from the garage at West Cairnbeg into the wash-house, thence into the house. He told the court that previously there had been no lock on that door and he hadn't done the job of fitting one until 12 July 1968—two months after the murder. This bore out my point about it not having been necessary that night to let anyone in to the house.

The joiner was the only witness called in my defence.

The lawyers made their speeches. People have often said to me that the speech given by Mr Lionel Daiches on my behalf was probably the finest of his career. The silver-tongued QC, they tell me, excelled himself and delivered a truly eloquent and poetic speech in defence of his client.

He ended with a famous quotation from the poet John Donne. ' "No man is an island, entire of itself; every man is a piece of the continent, a part of the main; . . . any man's death diminishes me, because I am involved in mankind; and therefore never send to know for whom the bell tolls; it tolls for thee. . . ."

'And for all of us,' he added.

Mr Daiches concluded 'I do not seek your pity, I ask only for a verdict in accordance with justice. I do not ask you, I *demand* that you return the verdict of Not Guilty.'

It was beautifully said, but it seemed so 'airy-fairy'! What did all this have to do with me? Far from being practical and down-to-earth it all sounded like a fine Shakespearean actor giving a perfect performance. But I was in the hands of these clever men. They knew their craft. They had prepared my defence and had done their best for me. As the court adjourned on the afternoon of 29 November I could only hope and pray that their best had been good enough to prove my innocence.

The jury had two days—all weekend—to stay at home and consider their verdict. Perhaps if they'd had to make their decision there and then, with the poetry of Mr Daiches's speech still ringing in their ears, the outcome might have been entirely different. Mr Dowdall thinks so; I will never know. I spent those two days in Craiginches waiting and wondering, still hoping for justice. There was little else to do. I slept. I was exhausted.

Monday dawned and Brian Tevendale, Alan Peters and I were driven in silence to Aberdeen High Court to hear our fate. Soon we would know what the jury had decided should happen to us.

The court gasped in astonishment when the verdict in the case of Alan Peters was announced.

'Not Proven.'

They had chosen to believe him rather than me.

I waited, trembling. I knew what the jury foreman would say next. The verdict in my case was indeed Guilty, by a majority verdict.

In the case of Brian, the verdict was unanimous.

'Guilty.'

I have no idea how I managed to walk down those sixteen steps from the dock. Mr Dowdall followed me, the tears streaming down his face. I didn't cry. I had to concentrate on making my legs work.

I can say truthfully from the bottom of my heart that if there had still been a death penalty I would at that moment gladly have gone to the gallows to be hanged. For at that moment I felt my life had ended. I was numbed. What lay ahead for me? Years and years in prison. A 'life' sentence. There was nothing more to live for and I wished to God I could die there and then. I remember thinking bitterly 'All these people who queued for hours with their flasks and sandwiches will be satisfied now! They've got what they wanted! They've seen a woman who has lived a life of wealth and comfort doomed to a life behind prison bars. All these people who laughed and tittered at the juicier bits of evidence—they'll all be pleased now. . . .'

As the pressmen raced from the court to file their stories and young Alan Peters walked out a free man, Brian and I were taken from the back entrance into a police van. We said nothing to each other during the journey back to Craiginches: we were both reeling with shock. When we arrived inside the prison gates I remember we were allowed a farewell kiss. Brian was handcuffed.

I was taken back to my cell to find that everything had been removed apart from the bed-frame. The governor was furious and ordered it all to be put back. I have no idea why everything had been taken out in the first place. I collapsed on that tiny, hard bed and cried and cried. There was no heart to break, for it was already in pieces.

The next day I was told Brian wanted to see me. We were allowed to talk through a glass partition while a prison officer watched us from a discreet distance. There was an obvious feeling of resentment between us. Little was said. What could there have been to say anyway? To reflect together on the morass of tangled emotions and contorted motives, to talk about who had done what and why was pointless now. To talk of what was to come, years and years in prison separated from everyone and everything we had known and loved, would have been like looking together across an endless, barren, desolate wasteland. There was only a glass partition between us, but in our thoughts we were a thousand miles apart.

Later that day my mother arrived to see me. Since that angry exchange of words that fateful Friday in August it was the first time we had spoken to one another. And again little was said. We cried together and embraced. We were both very upset.

The white police Jaguar sped swiftly southward through the pale, dreary December countryside. As we neared Greenock I saw the royal yacht *Britannia* anchored not far offshore in the Firth of Clyde. I wondered who was to board her: the Princess Margaret who had smiled at me as she danced the Paul Jones at Balmoral all these years ago, or the Prince Charles who had tugged playfully at his grandmother's pearl necklace?

Perhaps they would be heading for somewhere in the sun, enjoying their trip aboard the lovely ship as she sailed across the great, free ocean.

The police car stopped. We had reached our destination and I stepped out.

Before me were the great, grim, heavy doors of Gateside Prison.

10

The day I walked into Gateside Prison was cold, rainy and miserable. There wasn't even a hint of sunlight to soften the harsh outlines of the grim, red-brick building which at that time housed all Scotland's female prisoners. I walked through those great, thick doors with a heart heavy as lead and a soul empty of hope. The doors slammed behind me. I was now cut off from the outside world. I was 'inside'.

I had no conception what lay ahead of me or what prison life would be like. It wasn't long, however, before I began to grasp that the life I was to lead within the walls of that prison was one of total wretchedness. Entering Gateside Prison in those days was like stepping back into the Middle Ages.

I was taken into what was described as the 'reception area' of the prison and put into the 'dog box'. It was like being shut in a tiny wardrobe. I only had just enough room to stand up or sit down on a hard wooden bench, and I was left for half an hour in this cramped, wooden kennel. I later learned that one woman had been brought in to spend her first half hour in the 'dog box' and had thought that this was where she was to spend the rest of her sentence. She went berserk and tried to kick it down.

Eventually the door of the 'box' was opened and I was led into another part of the reception area to stand before a grim-faced prison officer. She gave me a look which left me in no doubt what was in her mind:

'So this is Sheila Garvie! We'll really put her through it. . . .'

The officer inspected my hair for lice. She then told me to stand in a nearby cubicle and to undress. The cubicle walls were only about three feet high. Apart from the prison officer, there were also two women prisoners working around the area at the time. At least during my three months in Craiginches I had been allowed my privacy, if little else.

I was given a sheet to wrap round myself, then told to drop it and stand naked while the officer's eyes moved over me.

I presumed that the reason for all this was to make certain I was carrying nothing with me. The purpose of it in my case was lost on me as I had already been in prison for three months. If I had been trying to conceal anything about my person it would most certainly have been found by this time!

I was issued with underwear—a bra, a cotton vest, a flimsy, brushed-nylon slip, a pair of nylon knickers and one pair of stockings. The shoes I was given looked quite new, but when I tried to put them on I discovered a nail sticking up half an inch through the heel. They were replaced by a very old pair which soon wore through the uppers. Nevertheless I wore those shoes all that first winter.

Then came a bright orange 'dress'. It was really an overall, which tied across the middle, but a prisoner soon learned never to refer to the Gateside 'dress' as an overall. My prison outfit was completed by the addition of a purple cardigan, and I remember thinking 'I must look a bonny sight!'

Every possession I had brought with me was taken away—my wedding ring, my watch, a pair of earrings. My morale was at rock bottom and I felt very disorientated.

I was then conducted along a stone-walled corridor. It was a dark, dismal, eerie place—almost ghostly, because I felt I could actually hear the breathing, the sad whisperings of all the women who had walked along it during all those years. I imagined that every woman who passed along that corridor added her own little piece of sadness to its chill atmosphere. The coldness I felt there had nothing to do with the dank December day outside.

At this time there were still male prisoners in Gateside, so I was taken through the huge, heavy iron gate which led into the women's section. The gate was locked behind me and I saw what was to be my new 'home' for the first time. It was a grim-looking prison hall surrounded by galleries. There were four tiers of cells, the top one about forty feet above the ground. I was put into an 'observation cell' on the ground floor for a little while, then taken to see the prison governor.

She was a fairly elderly, fine-looking woman with a charming manner. I recall little of the brief interview. I was later to learn, however, that behind that charming manner lay the hard-line views of a strict disciplinarian who was very popular with the prison staff because of her methods.

After the interview, I went back to my observation cell. It was much like other cells, only there was a hatch in the door through which a prison officer could look at any time, day or night. There was a bed with a straw mattress, a table, a chair and a small wardrobe. The room smelt badly and in the corner was a cracked, worn, plastic chamber pot. The back of the door looked as though it had taken a good battering over the years—as though bits of furniture had been thrown at it, in fact—and there were scratch marks on it made, I presumed, by women who couldn't stand being locked up.

During the first three weeks, to make matters worse, all the furniture was removed from my cell at night, leaving me only with my bed and the chamber pot.

The first night was like many, many nights that were to follow. For my first three weeks in the observation cell, the light was left on at night which made it difficult to sleep. But that was by no means the worst thing about the nights at Gateside.

The sobbing, the screaming went on endlessly. Women cried and shouted and battered on their cell doors. It was like being in a strange hell on earth and I began to think I had been put in a mental hospital instead of a prison. One woman in particular screamed for hours every night. God knows what nightmares she was having.

One night, as I lay sleepless listening to this bedlam, I heard a terrible struggle going on along the corridor. A cell door was opened and someone was dragged out and along to the 'padded cell', which was only two doors away from mine. This cell never seemed to be empty. If it wasn't occupied by one of the women prisoners, one of the young Borstal girls was in there. It was heart-rending to hear the screams of a woman who had been put into that cell, for she would be thrown in naked with only a blanket tossed after her.

There was a 'silent' cell too, a punishment cell for women who had been caught fighting, perhaps. That was hardly ever empty either.

During those three weeks in the observation cell I was allowed out to eat and was escorted by a disciplinary officer to the sewing room to work. I knew I was going to have a hard time with the staff because of who I was, but I was grateful— and always will be—to Gateside's Glaswegian inmates who looked after me right from the start. They had hearts of gold and watched over me in those early days like mother hens. They told me that had Trudy Birse come into Gateside they would gladly have thrown her from the top gallery!

After my three weeks under observation I was interviewed, as was normal practice, by a psychiatrist. I told him I now wanted to be treated like any other woman prisoner. I was moved to a cell on the first floor, then later to one on the top gallery, which was reserved for long-sentence prisoners serving more than eighteen months. (Those serving less than eighteen months were usually shoplifters, women who had been convicted of breach of the peace or prostitutes who had been caught soliciting.)

When they moved me to the first floor, I complained that I had not been allowed a bath in three weeks. Soon after that, it was decreed that long-sentence women would be allowed to bathe twice a week.

During those first few weeks in jail Brian Tevendale and I exchanged letters, and in one of the first he told me he had written to the Secretary of State for permission to marry me. He wanted me to do the same. But I never did. I had no intention ever of marrying Brian Tevendale while we were in jail, because I knew it was pointless, would serve no purpose and would give neither of us any happiness. Those thousands of people who were told by the newspapers at the time that we both wanted to be married were misled. I never asked to marry Brian.

After I had made it clear that I had no intention of asking the Secretary of State if we could be married, I stopped writing to Brian and requested that I be given no more letters from him if any should arrive.

The first year in Gateside Prison was quite simply a nightmare. Many, many times I wondered how I could commit suicide. I thought about drowning myself in the bath, and considered also how I might kill myself with a knitting needle. I know that some of the other women felt the same way.

Our day began at 5.45 a.m. when we were wakened in our cells. The door was opened at 6.15 by which time we had to be dressed and ready to carry our chamber pots to the 'slop out'. I had to hold my breath during this early morning chore, for the stink in the place was terrible and if I hadn't managed to stop my breathing for the time it took to empty the pot and get out I would probably have vomited. After this ordeal, we had to collect a jug of water—usually lukewarm— to take to our cells for washing. This small quantity of water had to be used for washing everything: yourself, your hair and your underwear—which had to be hung out on the gallery rails every night. The clothes were still damp the next morning. It was impossible to keep yourself both clean and dry from day to day.

Then the hall bell would ring, and we were lined up and marched into the dining room for breakfast. There was porridge, and perhaps a piece of sliced sausage or a small slice of cheese. Occasionally we would get a spoonful of jam to go with the two slices of bread and margarine. The amount of milk in the plastic cup just covered the bottom and no more.

Once a week we got an egg. It came hard-boiled and without a spoon to eat it with. You had to peel off the shell and squash it between the slices of bread. One morning I took my courage in both hands, got up from my table and went to the counter to ask one of the cook-officers for a spoon with which to eat my egg. The whole dining room fell silent. I felt like Oliver Twist asking for more. . . .

The officer looked at me as though I had asked for either the moon or a bag of gold. She was struck dumb for a few seconds, then turned to another officer with whom she had a conference. I can still remember the look of disbelief on their faces as they discussed what to do with this woman who had asked for a spoon. My face was scarlet, but I was determined. Was it so much to ask, to have a spoon with which to eat an egg?

The officer then turned sharply and said in a loud, strident voice 'Give the lady a spoon to eat her egg!'

I got my spoon and I ate my egg with it, but when our eggs were handed out the following week, there were still no spoons. I didn't persevere.

We all started work at 8.00 a.m. Wages were 3s 6d a week, which was just enough to buy half an ounce of tobacco and some cigarette papers to 'roll your own'. There was the sewing room, the cookhouse and the laundry room, or you could spend the day cleaning up in the reception area or laying out clothes for a woman who was to appear in court.

Work in the sewing room meant day after day of relentless monotony, for all we were usually allowed to make was sheets, pillowslips or handkerchiefs—sewing for hours on end in straight lines.

There was a short break at 10.00 a.m. and we were allowed a cup of what was described as tea, but was practically undrinkable. They didn't allow smoking during the mid-morning break and there was nothing to eat. We then worked on until 12.30, when we were marched back into the dining room for lunch.

The standard of the vegetable soup, which we were given every single day of our prison lives, depended on which prisoner had cooked it. The cook-officers in the kitchen spent most of their time sitting around drinking coffee and talking. After the soup came fish, or macaroni, or sometimes meat, all with potatoes. A large amount of the food went into buckets to be taken away by a local farmer to be fed to his pigs.

One of the most common 'pigswill' sweets was prunes and semolina, which was nicknamed 'wallpaper paste'. We usually ate the prunes, but most of the 'wallpaper paste' went into the bucket for our animal friends. One day, as usual, I threw the remains of mine—including the prune stones—into the bucket and got up to leave. A few seconds later an officer yelled 'Who threw the stones into the bucket?' I came forward to admit to this crime.

'Take that bucket and pick out every single prune stone!' she said. 'The prune stones choke the pigs!'

The trouble was that, as I soon discovered, everyone else had thrown their prune stones into the bucket as well, so it was a long and messy job.

After lunch we would be taken out to walk in the exercise yard for an hour. We walked in two circles, the inner circle for first offenders and the outer one for those with previous convictions. I was, naturally, in the inner circle. We walked round and round for the whole hour and by the end of the exercise period I was so dizzy I could hardly stand up straight.

You could talk quietly with the person you were walking with if you wanted to, but laughing was not allowed—and any woman prisoner caught looking up at the windows of the men's cells was put on report!

At tea time, about 4.30 in the afternoon, we were given more of the terrible tea and a couple of slices of bread and margarine. If you couldn't eat the bread and tried to pass one of the slices to someone who was hungrier, you would be put on report.

Occasionally we were treated to a tea time 'special', which we called 'jam fritters'. Gateside jam fritters consisted of two half-slices of bread with jam in the middle, dipped in a tasteless batter and deep fried. They were revolting. The fat in the pans wasn't changed from one month to the next.

After tea, at about 5.00 p.m we were all locked in our cells again, although we were allowed out a little later to collect another jug of water. Recreation in the evenings was regarded as a privilege and was only allowed to prisoners who had been 'inside' for at least two months. For those first two months, therefore, I remained locked in my cell from five o'clock until the following morning.

At 8.30 in the evening we were allowed out of our cells for a few minutes to hang our washing on the rails and were given another cup of tea and more bread. Soon after that it was 'lights out'—and the screaming and the sobbing started again. The cells were freezing cold during the winter nights and I soon learned one trick at least to try and keep a little warmer in bed. I collected old newspapers, laid them between the thin blankets and tried to make a 'nest' on the hard straw mattress.

The worst days were Sundays. After tea at 4.00 p.m. we were locked away in our cells with our chamber pots until the next morning.

One morning at 6.45 I was taken from my cell by a prison officer and led to the 'slop-out'. An old 'wino' had spilt her chamber pot all over the floor and it was awash with urine. The smell was terrible. They ordered me to clean it up; I did so. Later in my cell, alone, I cried and cried. But I would not allow one tear to drop in front of those officers: I wouldn't give them the satisfaction of seeing me upset.

For three months during my first year in Gateside I worked in the kitchen, from 6 a.m. until 6 p.m. This made prison life slightly more bearable for at least I had the chance to try my hand at cooking, which I enjoyed—and I got a few compliments from fellow prisoners. But there were draw-backs. Kitchen work was back-breaking, because it meant scrubbing floors and cleaning the antiquated equipment. My stint in the kitchen ended, in any event, when I had to be taken to Greenock Royal Infirmary to have an ulcerated mole removed. On my return, it was back to the long hours in the monotony of the sewing room.

I tried to be a model prisoner, for I knew that because of my background and the publicity which had attended my trial prison officers were just watching and waiting for me to step out of line. However, discipline was harder than I ever imagined it would be and there was no communication whatsoever between prisoners and officers.

Prisoners were allowed to take books from the prison library twice a week, although the reading material provided by the authorities consisted largely of cheap romantic trash about doctors and nurses falling in love and living happily ever after. There were one or two decent books, however, some of which I read and re-read rather than dull my brain

119

with the slushy novels. I shunned the 'recreation' periods—which consisted of an hour or so of television or the chance to hear old pop records on a gramophone—and kept very much to myself, reading in my cell instead. I found myself 'on the carpet' one day for doing this. I was given a severe talking-to by the prison matron for my lack of communication with prison officers and my tendency to keep to myself.

I told the matron I could not communicate with them because their attitude and the whole atmosphere of the place made any civil contact with a prison officer impossible. They were just bitches. I left her office unchanged in my attitude, for I knew I hadn't broken any of the rules and there was nothing they could do to me to make life any worse than it was.

The nearest I ever got to being put on report, in fact, was one memorable day in the sewing room when I and another woman had decided to have a fly cigarette because there were no officers there at the time. An officer came into the room, her nostrils twitching at the smell of smoke, and I could see she was out for blood.

'Who's been smoking?' she yelled.

I felt I had nothing to lose, and I couldn't have cared less by this time if they'd locked me up in the 'dog box' for a year. Going on report merely meant the loss of the recreation privilege, or being locked in your cell for three days without any reading material. What did it matter any more?

I stood up. There were about fifteen women in the room at the time, most of them Glasgwegians. They all promptly stood up as well! The whole of the sewing room was on its feet and the officer was flabbergasted. Her face was scarlet with rage, for she knew she couldn't put us *all* on report. She hastily discussed the situation with a civilian officer, following which we were all marched into an office and given a stern warning.

I shall always be grateful to all those women who stood up that day.

I kept myself to myself and never discussed what had happened to me with anyone, feeling very withdrawn from my fellow prisoners. Often, however, they would bring their problems and their secrets to me—secrets which I shall always keep—and tell me of their lives and of the circumstances which had brought them into Gateside Prison.

Most of my fellow inmates had led very hard lives, but there were few 'hard women' in Gateside. They were the sad, lonely rejects of society without the strength to break away from the wretched circumstances of their lives. As they talked, often every second word was a swear word, for many of them had had little or no education and to curse and swear was the only way they knew of expressing themselves.

I soon learned that background and education were unimportant in the face of kindness, trust and the willingness to help and comfort others. Many of these supposedly 'hard' women—prostitutes, drunks, thieves—would have done anything for me. They trusted and respected me for they knew that if ever I witnessed anything that was against prison rules I would never 'squeal' to any of the officers. There were those, of course, who did—to curry favour and privileges for themselves—and they were shunned by the rest of us.

The other group of women who were hated and despised by all, including myself, were women who were serving sentences for crimes against children. Women who had hurt, ill-treated, neglected or killed a child were treated like lepers, avoided and loathed by their fellow prisoners. They were often spat upon, and if the other women had had their way they would have been lynched. Most of us had been separated from our own young ones and the fact that another woman could do harm to a child brought out a communal aggressive maternal instinct in us all. I was continually aware that prisoners hated the way officers bent over backwards to protect those women and make their lives easier.

I remember one woman who was serving her sentence for killing her child through neglect. She appeared to me a person without any feeling and without the ability to grasp what she had done, or to distinguish between good and evil. She should have been in a mental hospital, not a prison. Often, she would try and talk to me. All I could ever bring myself to say, however, was 'I feel sorry for you!'

In May 1969, six months after I began my sentence, my

mother died. I had been allowed to visit her in Stonehaven near the end of her painful illness, but I was not allowed to attend her funeral. I then began to suffer torments of worry about the future of my children. I spent many of the hours alone in my cell wondering and worrying if they would be all right and if the trustees would appoint the right person to care for them. It was a bad time.

Altogether, that first year in Gateside Prison was a living nightmare. Prisoners were consistently humiliated, degraded and treated like animals. Prison officers used to stand at the bottom of the gallery and scream at us, and I am convinced that some of those officers in the early days would have thrived under the Nazi regime. Most of them agreed on the re-introduction of capital punishment and I wouldn't doubt that if someone in authority had decided to bring back the rack they would have applauded the decision with malicious glee.

Room searches were a regular event, and there was no respect whatsoever amongst these officers for your few little possessions. I would go back to my cell to find everything strewn in a heap in the middle of the floor.

There was so little to cling to in those days, even the smallest, most unimportant thing by 'outside' standards became more valuable to you than gold. I remember after one of these searches nearly weeping when I saw they had callously thrown a little potted plant on the floor, scattering the plant and the earth from the pot. It was a sad day too, when my straw mattress was replaced by a new one. I had grown almost to love that mattress, in which I had moulded myself a 'nest' in the hard-packed straw. Now I had to start all over again and make another nest comfortable enough to sleep in.

I could feel myself beginning to sink with the rest, for a human being can only take so much misery and humiliation before it becomes easier just to accept the situation and become a zombie rather than to fight and try to retain some self-respect. I know without any doubt that if I had been compelled to spend the ten years of my sentence in this kind of prison I would now be a human vegetable, for a system like

122

that must have created in a long-serving prisoner a creature so degraded and institutionalised that the tiniest remaining spark of human hope and pride would have been doused forever. I would have been alienated from the rest of the world for the rest of my life.

Within that first year Lady Martha Bruce, who had been Assistant Governor of Gateside when I arrived, was appointed to the post of Governor. I could not have guessed at the time how important this was to be to me.

She started doing a daily round with the prison matron and when she came into the sewing room we all had to stand. Like the other prisoners I was now so hostile towards any form of authority I resented this deeply. Why should we have to stand up when this woman came into the room? I never looked at her: I either stared past her or looked away in another direction. I was trying to insult her by refusing to meet her gaze, but I was conscious of her looking at me and if, on occasion, our eyes met by accident for a split second, I had the feeling that she was trying to say 'Keep your chin up!'

To a certain extent those looks of encouragement across the sewing room from the new governor helped me, but I had got to the stage of being prepared to sink with the rest and I resented Lady Martha trying to stop me.

I didn't know it then, but a wind of change was destined to blow through the dreary halls of Gateside Prison. At first it was only a gentle breeze, but in the years to follow it was to gather strength.

A year or so after I began my sentence it was arranged that I should meet my three children outside the prison—at a clinic near the centre of Glasgow. The arrangements had been made by a psychiatrist after 'talk sessions' with the long-serving prisoners, supervised by a senior officer. I remember we were all very awkward at these sessions and few of us could think of anything to say: certainly nothing very constructive.

During one of the 'talk-ins', I suddenly got this terrible urge to burst out laughing and I tried desperately to think of something to stop me. The only thing I could think of was colours: I thought about different shades of red, green, blue, yellow and concentrated hard to keep my mind off my uncontrollable desire to start giggling.

Then the psychiatrist talking to us that day asked me 'Sheila, what are you thinking about?' I told him. 'Colours, just different colours. . . .'

I must have said the right thing at the right time, for within a week the meeting with my children had been arranged.

Lady Martha Bruce told me that a psychiatrist had suggested it might be a good idea for me to see the children outside the prison environment. Meetings between prisoners and their children were usually organised to take place in the previous governor's home, which had by this time been converted, and I had seen my son Robert two or three times there. This time, however, we were to meet far away from the prison walls and I was excited and happy about the prospect of seeing the children in an ordinary environment.

The day arrived and I was driven from Greenock into Glasgow and taken to a clinic tucked away in a quiet terrace just off busy Sauchiehall Street.

The meeting was a disaster. The news that Sheila Garvie was to meet her three children at the clinic had somehow 'leaked' to the press and what had originally been intended as a quiet few hours for a mother to spend with the children she missed so much turned into a circus. Dozens of pressmen gathered outside, and although the children were smuggled out safely past the reporters and photographers, I myself was 'besieged' inside for several hours.

Finally a plain-clothes detective worked out a way of getting me out. The two of us would walk from the back of the clinic with our arms around each other like a courting couple and quietly get into a car which had been brought to the rear entrance. The trick worked, and I was driven back at last to Gateside, heartbroken and angry that the meeting I had longed for so much had been ruined.

That was the last time—more than ten years ago—that I saw my two daughters.

Back in Gateside, Lady Martha was beginning to make

the regime easier, but there was still a long way to go before life in prison became tolerable.

Lady Martha introduced group discussions, chaired by an officer, at which we were allowed to air our views and complaints. The first thing I brought up was the question of our underwear, which was still damp every morning even after hanging on the gallery rails all night. After that discussion we got a full change of underwear, two of everything. Lady Martha then introduced a leisure dress and shoes for visits and recreation and told us we would be allowed to receive parcels of soap and cosmetics. This last privilege, however, was stopped in its early stages after one woman was sent drugs in her parcel.

Towards the end of my first year in prison I had started a correspondence course in hotel and catering management from a school in London. I completed the course ten months later. It was little comfort, but the work had occupied my mind and had given me a goal to strive for and something to cling to.

Just before Christmas in my second year in Gateside the education officer, who worked mainly with the young Borstal girls, asked me if I would like to try for an 'O' grade in dressmaking and design. I decided to have a go, although we didn't have much time left to study, as the exam was in the spring. She persuaded four other long-sentence women to try for the 'O' grade as well. I passed, then started working for Highers in English, home economics, secretarial studies—typing and audio—and dressmaking and design.

There was no doubt that the staff deeply resented this new education programme. Many of them were so uneducated themselves that I think they felt ill at ease with prisoners with some academic ability and annoyed that any of us should try to better ourselves. The staff preferred uneducated prisoners, for they could treat them as they liked. I remember one day standing beside an 'old timer' who had been in and out of the prison many times. A senior officer was asking sarcastically 'Well, what are you in for this time, dear, an 'O' grade or a Higher?'

All who were Gateside prisoners at the time will remember

the summer of 1970. There was a severe water shortage in Greenock and we were allowed only one bath a week instead of two, with only enough water to cover the bottom of the bath. One afternoon, the sewing-room officer told me that restrictions had been lifted as the shortage was over. I was as excited as a child with a new toy. Now I could go and have a good hot bath and feel really clean again after six weeks of trying to bathe in an inch or so of water!

Another woman and I ran to the washroom and turned on the taps and it was wonderful to see all that lovely water gushing into the baths, knowing that now we could have a really good soak.

Then suddenly the sound of a loud, harsh voice stopped short our childish glee. An officer had come into the room and she was saying angrily 'What do you think you are doing, Sheila Garvie? I haven't been given any instuctions to lift bathing restrictions! Let that water out!'

I couldn't believe my ears. We had to pull out the plugs and stand there while all the water ran away. Discipline with reason I could understand, but discipline of that irrational kind was just pure badness.

Neither will any of us forget the Christmas of 1971. On Christmas Eve we heard on a news broadcast that this year the women of Gateside were to get a very special orange sweet with their festive dinner the next day. We were all very excited about this. What delights, we thought, had the cook officers come up with for our Christmas dessert? The radio reporter assured us that it was to be a delicious orange concoction.

The next day it arrived on our plates. It was an apology for a sponge, with layers of margarine and sugar and a slice of fresh orange on top. It tasted horrible. I wish that radio reporter could have heard the thuds as the 'delicious orange concoction' was hurled into the buckets for the pigs by disgusted and disappointed prisoners.

When I had been in prison about three years—I can't remember exactly when—I was allowed out for the first time (with an officer). We went to Largs to spend a couple of hours walking around the town. I had saved up a little money from

126

my 'earnings' and bought a small piece of material to make myself a blouse, for by this time we were no longer restricted to sewing sheets and pillowcases. My most vivid memory of that day out is the wonderful fresh smell of the sea and the seagulls flying over the water. I wonder now if those short trips 'outside' were really of any permanent value, for although just a couple of hours in a seaside town was like a short-term paradise at the time, it only made it a lot harder to return to prison.

Back 'inside', however, conditions were improving steadily. We were now allowed to brush our teeth at the sinks, and we weren't locked up in our cells for such long periods as before. Lady Martha had also introduced a choice of menu and those of us serving long sentences were now allowed to eat in a corner of the chapel out of the constant gaze of prison officers. Morale was slightly higher and communication between staff and prisoners was better than before—it could hardly have been worse! New staff started to come in, and under Lady Martha's influence the rest of the staff were compelled to change their hard-line attitudes.

I had been put in charge of the library on the top gallery, the one reserved for long-sentence prisoners.

I feel now that the strict discipline of my early life with a stern Scottish father had helped me in many ways to come through the very worst of Gateside Prison.

We had visits from experts. I remember the day one of them arrived at Gateside to chat with some of us. I believe this particular woman is regarded as a leading expert on social problems in general—and is thought to have great insight into the effects of prison life on female inmates.

She talked at great length about her marriage and how wonderful it was, and went on to describe the beautiful wedding her daughter was soon to have.

She turned suddenly to me and said 'Of course, Sheila, you'll miss all that with your daughters, won't you?'

It was like a knife through the heart. My grief at being separated from the children was intensified. My pillow was sodden for many nights, but eventually I stopped crying.

Tears became a luxury and I envied women who wept, for my tears had just dried up and I could only cry inside.

Three years after my sentence began the top gallery of the prison was painted, and I was given the use of an extra cell, next to my own, in which I could study. There was a desk and two chairs and I was allowed a small electric cooker. I could now make my own tea.

About the same time I was given the unenviable task of looking after the prison governor's hens. Perhaps they thought that my farm background made me an expert in such matters, but in fact the only contact I ever had with the birds at West Cairnbeg was to help collect the eggs when the hen man was on holiday. However, I agreed eagerly to take on the task, for it meant I would be free from exercise periods and at least I would no longer have to walk around in circles for an hour each day.

During the setting-up of the project I remember watching with great amusement the gardening officer kneeling on the ground intently trying to figure out the construction of the hen houses, with the eyes of two male prisoners intently riveted on her posterior. . . .

The hens duly arrived. About ten dozen eggs were sold to prison officers every week and the profits went to buy material for tweed pinafore dresses for long-sentence prisoners. Not all the eggs were sold to staff, of course: some were sneaked into my study cell as ingredients for pancakes and I would occasionally steal the odd onion from the prison vegetable garden to make Spanish omelettes for myself and a few of my fellow long-term inmates. I was responsible for those hens until we moved to Cornton Vale three and a half years later and am proud to say that during that time only one or two of them died.

Just before Christmas 1972 I received a letter from my children's trustees telling me that in their opinion my son's visits to me were doing him very little good, and that they no longer thought it wise that he should come and see me. It was a terrible letter and I was very near to a breakdown when I realised that those precious interludes with my little boy were to be stopped. I have not seen him since.

Not long afterwards, however, a woman psychologist in Stirling contacted Lady Martha to ask her if she thought any of the women prisoners would be interested in trying to design a book for mentally-handicapped children. I was asked if I would like to try my hand at designing and making a prototype book for those youngsters and I agreed.

I designed two, big, easy-to-handle picture books which I called *Come Play With Me*, made of different materials like fur, wool and velvet, and constructed so they could be taken apart and put together again. They were intended to help the children to identify different shapes and textures and to learn simple tasks, like fastening buttons and zips.

I asked women prisoners who were having their hair cut to give me the hair. I wanted to include a section in the book in which the children could insert a hair grip into 'real' hair on the picture of a little girl. I got so much hair I could have started a wig factory! At the same time I also made a construction doll with detachable limbs.

The psychologist in Stirling was kind enough to send along a picture of a little mentally-handicapped boy playing with my book some time later, and I believe they were very pleased with it.

On many occasions, too, I was asked by the governor to lay on buffets for visitors to the prison. The cook-officers got the credit, but I enjoyed a good tuck-in when no-one was looking!

The most traumatic event of my whole prison life happened during the last full year at Gateside Prison.

I had talked occasionally to one of the young Borstal girls who had been sent into the women's section at Gateside because she hadn't been responding to treatment. She had been put in what they called the hospital wing, which was really only a glorified larger cell in the hall.

She had told me that her mother was a prostitute in Dundee and had revealed during our few short conversations details of the dreadful background she'd come from and the awful life she had led. I felt very sorry for her. She was just a child—only about sixteen—and she'd never had a chance in life.

One evening, the gallery at Gateside was almost deserted, for everyone had gone to see a film in the chapel. I rarely went to 'cinema night' as I preferred to read in my study cell. I could move about freely as I wasn't locked up.

There was only one other person in the hall that night, another woman prisoner who had decided to stay behind and wash her hair instead of going to see the film with all the others.

The whole place was silent. It was almost eerie with no-one about, and you could have heard the proverbial pin drop as I sat at my books. I got up to go to the toilet—and nearly dropped in my tracks with shock when I saw what was happening outside. The young Borstal girl was hanging, literally by her fingertips, from the rail on our top gallery, forty feet above the tiled floor of the hall below!

I couldn't believe what I was seeing at that moment. I ran back into my cell, terrified, and shut the door. My thoughts were racing madly as I told myself 'This can't be happening!'

Then something inside me said 'Get out there and help that kid!'

I ran outside again. She was still there, hanging from her fingertips, and below was a long, long drop to death or very serious injury. I was scared to grab her in case she let go. Suddenly the voice inside me took over and I started shouting at her. I don't remember what I said—it was as though someone else was doing the talking for me—but I do recall getting angry and saying 'You think *you've* got problems; *I've* been in this place for nearly five years! What do you think you're doing?'

By this time the other woman who had been in her cell washing her hair had come out, and I yelled at her to go and get help.

Whatever I said to that young girl made her hang on, and perhaps I saved her life—I don't know. I persuaded her to get her feet on to the rail of the gallery below in the hope that she might drop down safely on to it instead of crashing forty feet down into the hall. By this time help had arrived and two officers (one the nursing officer) grabbed her legs and caught her as she slithered down. I was in a state of shock and had to be given a sleeping pill.

The incident was hushed up at the time, for the youngster should never have been left on her own that night, but I was asked to write a report on what had happened. I learned later that the girl had asked the other woman in the gallery that night if she could speak to me, and had been told not to bother me as I was studying. I also learned that she had been suffering from severe depression. To the end of my days I will never forget that young girl. She was so very young, and so very unhappy.

The soft breeze of change which had begun to waft through Gateside during those earlier years had now strengthened into a gale, thanks to the kindness and understanding of Lady Martha Bruce. It was easier, however, to boost the morale of the prisoners with the reforms she had instigated than to soften the hard-line attitude of the 'old guard' among the prison officers. They resented those reforms deeply and still 'hit back' from time to time with a word or a deed which smacked of the horrors of that first year.

In the early days officers had worn black uniforms which I thought made them look like bus conductresses. Latterly, they were issued with an outfit rather like an air hostess's, designed to give them a softer image. But underneath those smart outfits there still beat some hard hearts with a strong reluctance to conform to the new ways. One day during my sixth year at Gateside, I was suddenly sent for by two officers and my two cells were thoroughly searched. I was then told to strip. It was the most humiliating experience and my mind went back to that first day when I had had to drop the sheet and stand naked in front of the officer in the reception area.

I got down to my bra and pants, then one of the officers ran her fingers around my bra. I was speechless. I couldn't understand the reason for it all.

After tea the same day I was sent for by a principal officer who told me she thought I might have come to see her after what had happened—hinting, I think, that the officers had been given no orders to do what they did. However, during the next few days about ten strip-searches were done, as though they were intended to cover up what had happened to me.

Even in the most humiliating of circumstances, my friends the Glasgow women always seemed to find a reason to laugh. After some of them had been strip-searched they told me how they had hummed 'The Stripper' as they took their clothes off for the officers!

In the spring of 1975 I had stomach trouble. Every time I ate my stomach swelled, and I was taken to Greenock Royal Infirmary for tests. I had lost a whole stone in weight. The surgeon who saw me thought I might have some kind of blockage in the duodenum. To this day, however, I have never been told the results of those tests and I presume now the symptoms must have been due to some kind of nervous condition.

For two or three years we had heard that a new prison was being built at Cornton Vale, near Bridge of Allan in Stirlingshire. The first prisoners were to be moved from Gateside to their new 'home' in the spring of 1975.

There is nothing worse than an indeterminate sentence. For six and a half years I had been mixing with prisoners who were only in for thirty days, women who had been given eighteen months, women serving four years. It was very hard not to know, never to be told, how long I was likely to be in prison.

On a spring day in 1975 I left Gateside Prison for the last time, with only a fleeting backward glance. I wondered what this Cornton Vale would be like—and I wondered even more how many years I would have to spend there.

11

I was the first prisoner to be registered at Scotland's new women's prison. My prison number was 1/75.

I was in an 'advance party' of four who arrived at Cornton Vale along with ten of the best Borstal girls whose job it was to set up a little 'factory' for making teddy bears.

It was still a prison, but there were grass lawns, paths, and fields beyond the fence. My new 'home' wasn't a cell, it was a neat, compact, clean little room with big clear windows through which I could look at the fields and the hills in the distance. At first I felt I wanted to be back in a real 'cell' with a tiny, barred window because when I looked through the window of my room at Cornton Vale at the fields and the hills, freedom seemed much closer. Perhaps it would have been better not to have seen so much of the lovely world outside, for freedom was still a long way away. I loved to see the hills, but they were still on the other side of a fence I couldn't cross.

Everything at Cornton Vale was clean and white and new and I felt as though I was in a hospital. That spring and summer we sunbathed on the grass, and actually got sun-tanned! It was a beautiful summer and Cornton Vale was like a whole new world, thousands of miles away from the gloomy corridors, the cramped cells and the towering old galleries of Gateside. They were now just a dark nightmare in the past, a nightmare we all tried hard to forget.

At first I lived in 'Bravo' block, but on 4 June 1975 I was moved to what was to be my permanent home in 'Papa' block, a unit for long-term prisoners and a 'show' unit for visitors, who came from all over the UK and from abroad.

At the beginning I was put in charge of the vegetable garden and did most of the planting. Then, when I discovered I didn't have a permanent job to do, I asked if I could set up a home-produce business, making cakes, sponges, jams and chutneys to sell to staff. Profits went to prison funds. It turned out to be a good going concern, for when I left prison it was still going strong with someone else in charge.

There was no more screaming and sobbing at night. There was a high-security block and a punishment unit, but they were built well away from the other units, so if there was screaming we couldn't have heard it.

There were seven of us in 'Papa'. They called seven a 'crucial' number for prisoners living in their own unit. In my room there was a washbasin with a mirror above, a worktop at which I could study and where I could keep books and plants, and a comfortable bed with a foam mattress, warm blankets and a nice bright bedspread. I had an armchair, a good light to read by, and I could open my window. The only things that came with me from Gateside were a cabinet and the armchair which had been in my study cell.

There was a radiator in each room and we all had free access to the toilet, shower and bath. There was hot water, plenty of it, whenever you wanted it. I felt as though I was living in the lap of luxury after those six and a half years in Gateside.

The big grill gate at the end of the corridor was opened every morning at seven and we made our breakfast and cleaned our rooms. I drew up a rota so that everyone knew who was to do what and when, and we all took a great pride in keeping 'Papa' unit spotless and shining. Every day I went to the stores to collect the raw ingredients for our meals, which were cooked in the unit's own neat little kitchen.

Even in an environment like this, a new prison with a much calmer and more relaxed atmosphere than the old, there was bound to be friction from time to time. As cook, I had to make certain that everyone got exactly the same size of portion, otherwise tempers could have flared! The catering techniques reminded me a little of wartime, for I discovered that if I saved a little on margarine during the day I would have enough left to make biscuits to eat with supper in front of the TV at night.

We had a television lounge, to which the unit upstairs came during the early evening. Long-sentence prisoners had one television for fourteen; shorter-sentence women had to share a set amongst a larger number. After six and a half years almost completely cut off from the world—for I had watched little TV at Gateside—it was wonderful just to see a news broadcast.

Styles had changed, clothes had become more casual and hair styles, especially men's, were quite different. I became a *Crossroads* fanatic, although I never watch it now. We all saw the TV series *Within These Walls*, about life in a women's prison, and we all thought it was a load of rubbish! Life in prison was never like that! Television was allowed until 8.00 p.m., but if there was something special on—a play or a film perhaps which didn't finish until 8.30—we were allowed to stay in the lounge and watch it till the end.

In general, our unit worked very well. I could see, however, that if a more intelligent woman were to be put in a unit with six other women she couldn't communicate with, life could be very difficult and depressing indeed. The seven of us were stuck with one another and we had to get along. Of course, the inmates of 'Papa' block did change from time to time as women were released and others took their place.

The whole way of life was much more relaxed than in Gateside. Officers would sit and chat and a prisoner would often find an officer in whom she could confide and with whom she could discuss her problems. No longer was there a terrible hatred of authority, for staff, welfare officers and education people worked together for a purpose. The staff were probably a lot happier too. When rooms were searched, officers showed a great deal more respect for our belongings, for books and plants were only shifted around, never thrown on the floor. By this time the 'old guard' from Greenock were—thankfully—in the minority, and those who were still with us either had to fit in with the new-style prison and its methods or leave.

There were keep-fit classes and PT classes in the central

block at Cornton Vale, and prisoners could take classes in English, maths, typing—all sorts of subjects. A lot of women who had previously had little or no education were astonished and delighted when they managed to pass 'O' grade English or even Higher Maths! The education standards were very high; shelves in the sitting room of each unit were packed with books which were changed regularly. There was a little shop in which we could buy make-up, and prison officials arranged for a hairdresser to visit Cornton Vale once a week. We all began to feel like women again—and look like women too.

I got the shock of my life one day not long after we arrived when I spotted my hens! They had come with us from Gateside, but fortunately I didn't get landed with the job of looking after them for very long this time!

One problem which will never be eradicated from any women's prison, no matter how 'open' and progressive, is that of lesbianism. The subject was discussed quite openly at Cornton Vale, for prisoners had heard that it was rife in jails in England. Staff were quick to stamp out any signs of lesbian liaisons, but they happened more often amongst younger prisoners who were simply lonely and searching for some kind of affection. I was always on my guard.

Prisoners came and went, and Sheila Garvie stayed on. I worked for almost two years in the assessment centre for Borstal girls, and assisted prison officers in teaching the youngsters to sew and do craft and cane work. I enjoyed this, for I felt I was doing something worthwhile, and I was always mindful of that young girl at Gateside and the awful night when she almost killed herself.

Then, in June 1975, I was served with my first parole papers. I had to write down my reasons for thinking I could be released.

This is what I said:

'I must write of the matter which is of greatest importance to me and which has influenced my thinking on all aspects regarding my future. I am very much aware of having to live for the rest of my life with the consequences of my past and

I know that my family have suffered the repercussions. No matter how much I regret this, it is forever with me.

'I have given much thought to my relationship with my family when I am released. They are always in my thoughts and my sincerest wish is for their happiness and well-being. Nevertheless, the years of separation have taught me that I must make the greatest sacrifice a mother has to make, and that is never at any time to force my company on my children. I want to be available at all times if they wish to see me. I am willing to do everything in my power to help them if they need me, but I do not wish to intrude in their lives. I feel that my eldest daughter, now married, who writes to me regularly, has to the best of her ability accepted the past and that strong bonds of love and affection exist between us. And while, as I have said, I will never intrude on the lives of my children, as a mother I cannot do other than hope that it will be possible, in time, no matter how long it takes, to regain their respect.

'With regard to my father, I know that he would welcome me to his home, and while it would give me much comfort to be there with him I feel the risk of publicity which would adversely affect him and my children makes it impossible for me to join him. More and more now I realise how much I owe to my parents and especially during my imprisonment I have been greatly sustained by my father's unfailing concern for me and my family and by the certain knowledge that distance cannot divide us.

'During the years I have spent in prison I have had much time to think deeply over my past life and looking back I am conscious of a maturing process which has been going on and which seems to have helped me to rise from despair and self-accusation to an appreciation of a fuller and wider view of existence and to a gradual regaining of self-respect. I have a deeper understanding of life and its complexities and am very much aware and conscious of the suffering of other people. I now have a readiness and willingness to take whatever life outside has in store for me.

'I am indebted to members of staff who, with their advice, knowledge and encouragement have enabled me to develop skills and expand my interest in a number of fields: dress and design, cookery, secretarial studies.

'My study of the English language and literature has helped me to gain confidence, and particularly my study of literature has given me a deeper understanding and keener awareness of life. At eighteen I applied to enter nursing, having taken evening classes in first aid and home nursing. I did not pursue it further, however, on becoming engaged. Work as an occupational therapist interests me greatly. I have a keen desire to help the handicapped, possibly because I know that in a sense I myself now have a handicap, although not visible but one I must be prepared to cope with for the rest of my life.

'I intend to change my name, and this is one reason why it seems wise to me to choose to live in a large city rather than a small rural community. I feel that life in the West of Scotland could give me the anonymity I desire and help me to make a fresh start. I am willing to take any type of employment after my release but would hope eventually to find work both interesting and satisfying.

'From previous harrowing experience of press publicity I would prefer not to have "training for freedom" as this would almost inevitably lead to confrontation with newspaper reporters who would cause my family increased embarrassment and anxiety. This is my main reason for not wishing "training for freedom" and while I fully realise that adjusting to life in the community will present many difficulties I am eager and willing to cope. I feel that the prospect of release and release itself after a prolonged period of imprisonment will no doubt present me with many problems which will not disappear, nor will they be lessened by continued imprisonment.

'It is my fervent hope that I will soon have the opportunity to face the challenge. It may be difficult for one who has not served life imprisonment to fully understand the thoughts and feelings of shock and great remorse, the wild regrets, the loneliness, the separation from family, and all that goes with imprisonment which cannot ever be fully explained in words. But I fervently hope that I will receive consideration and understanding in making this representation.'

Normally, prisoners receive a reply to their plea for parole within six months, but the winter of 1975–1976 passed and I heard nothing. In March of 1976, I wrote to the Secretary of State.

'On June 23 1975 I submitted my first representation regarding parole. I have not yet received notification of the Parole Board's decision and I now write to you to express my deepest concern with regard to the prolonged delay. I would very much appreciate knowing what decision has been reached regarding my future. I should like to think that those who make these decisions understand to some extent the inner turmoil, the anguish of regret and remorse that has been constantly with me during my sentence and will be with me as long as I live. But surely those concerned with parole decisions will understand too that this prolonged period of waiting to know what decision has been reached has an extremely un-nerving affect which is hard to "thole".

'May I please, please, know your decision?'

In March, the same month, my second letter was acknowledged by a small card addressed to Sheila Garvie, prisoner 1/75. And that was all.

Twelve long months after I had applied for parole, I was told that my application had been turned down.

This aspect of the prison system is unbelievably cruel. For those twelve months I had waited in hope and had been told nothing. When the blow came it was a hard one. However, in the summer of that year, 1976, I was told I should write a second plea to the Parole Board. I composed another appeal. It said:

'It is now over a year since I wrote my first representation, the contents of which remain unchanged. Your decision I accept with deep regret and sad disappointment. During the prolonged and lengthy lapse of time awaiting your decision, my mind on many occasions has given way to despondency. Only my profound faith in God has sustained me through these months of waiting. It has strengthened my mind and given me added determination to overcome anxieties and difficulties which may face me in the future, difficulties which will not disappear or diminish by continued imprisonment. Since my transfer from Greenock to this healthier environment I have felt the benefit and appreciated the advantages of Cornton Vale and what it provides. At the beginning of my stay here I was given the responsibility of initiating a home-produce project which I managed successfully for months. I am proud to add it continues to flourish.

'My next move was to the Borstal assessment centre where I have worked for the past seven months. There, I assisted the officer in charge to instruct girls in a variety of handicrafts. The girls spend the first six weeks of their Borstal training at this centre. I find this type of work both satisfying and interesting. I gain much in helping the girls to make an item from start to finish, be it simple or more complicated. The interesting aspect of the work is that it is imaginative and seeing these girls enjoy creative activities, achieve results and hence gain confidence is rewarding to me.

'For these reasons I would very much like to extend my knowledge in this area of work on my release. In addition to my present work I am responsible for cooking the meals in the unit which I share with six other women. This work I do to the best of my ability.

'I fervently hope that the period of time taken to make a decision is considerably shorter than the last one.'

It was almost exactly one year later, however, when I was told that the Parole Board had reached its decision. But this time my application had been successful. Sheila Garvie would be released from Cornton Vale Prison in December 1978.

During all those years in prison I had endured many things. Looking back on those early days at Gateside Prison, I had thought the worst was over. But the long months of waiting for a Parole Board decision, during which no communication of any kind was sent to relieve the strain and agony of not knowing whether one is to be released, or when, was the worst thing I ever had to endure 'inside'. I hope that in the future the authorities will look more sympathetically on this aspect of our prison system, and understand more fully the feelings of those who wait for months on end for a decision.

140

That same summer I was allowed 'outside' on my own for the very first time. Legs trembling, I walked through the prison gates, and for the first ten minutes of my mile-and-a-half walk into Bridge of Allan I kept looking behind me to see if someone was following.

I bought cigarettes in a little shop and was served by a woman who had previously worked at Cornton Vale. 'Hello Sheila,' she said. 'How are you getting on?'

After I had been given a definite date for my release, something I had prayed would happen for so long, the days, weeks and months seemed to drag by even more slowly. I was working now in the staff canteen, situated outside the prison grounds, from 8 a.m. until 6 p.m. I was given a day off every week, usually on a Thursday, and was allowed to go back to 'Papa' Block a little earlier on Sundays. During the last twelve months of my imprisonment I was also allowed to go into Stirling, where I would walk around, look at the shops, have a cup of tea.

I travelled four times to Aberdeen to visit relatives, and I spent the Christmas of 1977 with an aunt and uncle who ran a small boarding house in the city. During my visits to Aberdeen I learned that they had decided to retire from the boarding-house business that September. They suggested I should take over when they left, and it was agreed by the prison authorities and the Parole Board that I should be released three months earlier to do so.

If this had not happened I would probably have been released as planned that December, most likely on the same day as Brian Tevendale.

There were no 'goodbyes' the day I left Cornton Vale for good. The curtain came down on almost ten years in prison in silence and secrecy. Only one or two senior prison officials knew I was going out, and the day before my release I worked in the staff canteen as usual. Staff and fellow prisoners assumed I was going on another three- or four-day trip to Aberdeen.

But this time I wouldn't be coming back.

I was dropped at Stirling Station by a prison officer that

morning and took the train north. I didn't feel nervous because I couldn't quite grasp the fact that this journey was very different from the others and I would not be travelling south again. My mind simply didn't take it in at the time.

Waiting for me on the platform in Aberdeen was a friendly social worker, who drove me to the lawyer's office to collect the keys of the little boarding house. We then went there, and stepped inside. A little later a few members of my family arrived and there was a quiet celebration. The evening passed, and they all duly left to go to their homes.

I was free at last. And alone.

12

On my way to Aberdeen earlier that day I bought a local
newspaper. My horoscope read: 'You have come to the end
of a confinement.' The freedom I had hoped and prayed for
through almost ten years of imprisonment was mine at last.

Freedom, as defined by one dictionary, is 'liberty of
action, the power of self-determination, independence of fate
or necessity. . . .' But for someone who has been imprisoned
for such a long time there are no words to describe the gift of
the return of freedom, which is the most precious possession
any human being can have.

In the early days, weeks and months after my release
from Cornton Vale, however, the gift of freedom was rather
like the gift of a complicated computer toy to a three-year-
old. I didn't know what to do with it, I had no idea how it
worked and it gave me little or no pleasure.

When it was time to do the shopping for myself and for
the guests in the boarding house, my social worker came to
collect me and drive me to the local supermarket. It was a
tremendous effort to go outside alone, and I couldn't face it.
For long hours I sat in my little bed-sitting room with its
warm gas fire and colour TV, trying to get used to the idea
that I was now free. At night I would suffer terrible dreams
about prison officers coming to take me back to prison.
During the day, I slowly began to realise that I was making
that cosy little sitting room into a new prison for myself.

I had lived in an artificial society for so long it was going
to take time and courage to cope with the normal one. For
the time being I was shutting myself away in a voluntary
imprisonment of fear and uncertainty.

Lord Byron describes the feeling much better than I can, in his poem *The Prisoner of Chillon*. The final verse, when the prisoner has at last been released, runs:

> And all my bonds aside were cast,
> These heavy walls to me had grown
> A hermitage, and all my own!
> And half I felt as they were come
> To tear me from a second home;
> With spiders I had friendship made,
> And watched them in their sullen trade,
> Had seen the mice by moonlight play,
> And why should I feel less than they?
> We were all inmates of one place,
> And I the monarch of each race
> Had power to kill — yet strange to tell,
> In quiet we had learned to dwell.
> My very chains and I grew friends
> So much a long communion tends
> To make us what we are; —
> And even I regained my freedom with a sigh.

Gradually, I began to venture out on my own. I was amazed that in the ten years since I had been in Aberdeen the volume of traffic had increased to such an extent that I was terrified to cross the road. I would walk hundreds of yards to the nearest crossing rather than risk my neck jay-walking like other pedestrians! The worst experience of all was crossing side streets with no zebra crossings or lights to help.

Some things I did enjoy. For months in prison I had dreamed of the things I would eat when I was finally released. I loved bacon and eggs for breakfast, and bought boxes full of black puddings—a craving that lasted for weeks!

Dealing with normal social contact was hard, however, and I found it almost impossible to carry on an everyday conversation with a neighbour or someone in a shop. Even now, eighteen months after my release, I still prefer the anonymity of the big, busy supermarket to the intimacy of the small corner shop where people are eager to chat.

During my ten years in prison, too, the country had switched over to decimal currency. I still thought in pounds, shillings and pence and found the new money system totally confusing. I could have been getting anything in my change in a shop. I never had any idea if it was the correct amount or not!

Making simple decisions, paying bills, getting my little car serviced, things which to others are a normal part of daily life were huge efforts for me. For years I had been told what to do, my life had been ordered and organised by others; my fate had been programmed in that strange artificial world and I'd had nothing to decide for myself. Any small decisions I had made during those ten years had been guided, dissected, refused or accepted by others. Now I had to stand alone and make decisions by myself, knowing that the rightness or wrongness of them rested in my own hands. I found it tremendously difficult to adjust. I often think now that a prison like Cornton Vale should have a flat or a hostel in the centre of a city, where long-sentence prisoners could live for a few months before final release. They could then get used to coping with a new, busy environment under supervision before they have to cope alone.

As I began to venture out gradually into the world I had left all those years ago, echoes of my past life in prison would pop up unexpectedly from time to time. Walking along George Street in Aberdeen I was greeted as a long-lost friend by a prostitute who had served time 'inside'! Then, during a trip to another large city, I decided to treat myself to a nice lunch, and deliberately picked a smart restaurant, thinking 'Surely there's no chance of me meeting anyone I know in here?' I chose a table in the corner and sat down. A cheerful waitress came over to take my order and as soon as our eyes met we knew we had both been in prison at the same time!

The girl smiled and whispered 'How are you getting on, Sheila? It's great to see you!'

My face was scarlet. She was the last person I had expected to see in the snooty atmosphere of this city-centre dining place!

There is a strong bond between former prisoners. You feel an immediate affinity towards someone you know has suffered at least to some extent the same fate as yourself.

When my order of steak and chips arrived it was mountainous, for my former fellow inmate had sneaked me a double helping from the kitchen. She served me with a quiet smile and I tucked in to the biggest plateful of steak and chips I have ever seen!

When I left prison, I had wanted to see Brian Tevendale again. He was released from prison in December 1978, three months after I was. I was advised against attempting such a meeting, however, for I was told the authorities would frown upon it. In any case, I knew by this time that he had been seeing someone during his trips outside and had formed a relationship with her.

Whether we would have had anything to say to one another I have no idea, but I did want to see him. I felt—and still feel—that for us not to meet after all that happened is rather like a story without an ending. But I hope now that he has found happiness in his new life and joy with his new love.

In the spring after my release I married in haste a young Rhodesian called David McLellan, a guest at my boarding house. I was lonely, afraid of the world, and desperately needed someone to lean on. I was deeply attracted to this young man, thirteen years my junior, and sincerely hoped that our marriage would be a chance for real happiness in the future.

I was wrong. After only eight months the marriage ended in violence and bitterness and at the time of writing I am seeking a divorce.

I met David only four months after my release, when I was very naïve and even more vulnerable. If the same man had arrived at my door looking for lodgings now, more than a year later, I would probably have regarded him very differently and acted with more perception. But, as they say, I must repent at leisure. I regret my mistake now—and hope for happiness for him too.

It is only now, after eighteen months of freedom, that I am gradually beginning to adjust properly to a 'normal' existence. I have, however, endured the depths of despair in my lifetime, and enjoyed the heights of happiness, and I doubt sincerely if I will ever be able to lead an ordinary life again, or feel at one with people whose lives have not been marred by the most awful of tragedies. All I hope for is a little security—and that other precious gift, peace of mind. Whether I will ultimately be blessed with that, I do not know.

It may have been a conscious process, or a sub-conscious one—I am not sure—but many of the most traumatic events of my past life have been blotted out from my mind. Yet the regrets remain, and always will. More than any woman, I am acutely aware of the dangers and foolishness of straying from a marriage and of falling in love with someone else. It happens to thousands of people, but in my case the contorted combination of circumstances ended in tragedy. Pent-up emotions exploded in violence—and a man died.

I had no hand in my husband's murder, but I deserved my sentence because I failed to halt the tide of events which led inexorably to his death. I was weak. I could have 'opted out' of the terrible tangle which resulted in the killing of Max Garvie, but I didn't. I carried on. I know now I have the kind of strength which got me through those terrible days in Gateside, but when I am involved with a man I am weak. My commitment is total and I am 'taken over' by the strong, domineering type of personality to which I am attracted.

My deepest regret, with me every hour of every day, is for the effect the tragedy of my husband's murder had on the young lives of my children. I love them dearly still, and hope with all my heart that what happened that night twelve years ago—and all the things that have happened since—will not mar their future happiness. My greatest hope of all is that some day I shall see them again. Whether or not this will ever happen I do not know. The decision is theirs and theirs alone.

Perhaps I can best record my present feelings by quoting part of a letter I wrote to my children's trustees, just after I had been told that they had stopped the visits of my young son while I was in Gateside Prison.

'I know only too well that the highest, greatest and most lasting values in life cannot be bought with money, but can be gleaned from life's bitter and harsh experiences.

147

'Perhaps those of us who realise how far we have strayed from what we could have been, from what we should have been; perhaps only those of us who through our own faults, our own mistakes, have endured the deep abyss of loneliness, regret, self-recrimination and separation from those who are dearest to us are capable of becoming more sensitive to the fears, anxieties and sufferings of others.

'Perhaps those of us who realise how far we have fallen know too the strength which comes from attempting to rise again.'

Postscript
by Laurence Dowdall

Statements and Precognitions

On the day when I first heard Sheila Garvie's story, in Craiginches Prison, I had taken with me the three conflicting statements made by the three accused to the police. I have never read such diametrically opposed versions of the same event. There was no way of reconciling them: only one could be the truth.

Tevendale's story read as follows:

'I met Maxie Garvie on the Scottish National Party outing to Bannockburn. I had a few drinks with him and his wife and was invited flying next day. On the following weekend I went down to the Marine Hotel in Stonehaven with him and his wife and when we left the Marine I sat in the back of his car with his wife at his request. When we arrived at the chip shop he and the front passenger . . . went into the fish shop. I followed and was promptly told to get back into the car and keep his wife happy. The weekend following I was invited up to the farm. We went out on Saturday night drinking. We had a few drinks when we returned home to the farm and I went to bed. A short time later Sheila was pushed into the room and the door was shut. She said she had been told to spend the night in there or else. Later on that week Sheila came down to the garage and picked me up from my work. She said Max wanted us to go out for a drink that night. When we arrived there he handed me the keys of the car and told me to take Sheila out as he was going out with someone himself. This happened a few weeks running. On three successive Saturdays, is that the right word, successive?

we went to Edinburgh and Glasgow and Edinburgh again spending the weekend in various hotels. On one particular night when I was out with Max himself he started making strange advances. At the time I was driving the car and I pulled up at the side of the road and told him that if he did not stop I would belt him. He laughed this off as if it were a joke. When we reached Cairnbeg we had a few drinks again in the house and I went upstairs to bed. Shortly after I was in bed he came in and sat on the edge of the bed. He was wearing a red-coloured dressing gown which was open and he was naked underneath. I told him if he did not leave the room I would get up, dress and walk home. He again laughed and left the room. One Saturday night Sheila, Max and myself had been drinking in Laurencekirk. When we returned home he suggested it would be a good idea to toss up to see who slept with Sheila that night. Sheila objected and was told to shut up. He tossed the coin and I won. He went through to sleep in the room that I usually had. About six o'clock in the morning I woke up and found that he was also lying in the bed with Sheila and I. Sheila later told me he had tried to have kinky sex with her when he first came in. She refused and he was scared the noise would wake me up. He once told me that he loved me more than he loved Sheila. He often offered me pills of various shapes and sizes which he usually took himself when drinking in the house. I once flew with him from Fordoun flying field to Bervie shooting up vehicles on the way. We were both severely intoxicated. When we landed he told me he was going to try out a new variation in homo-type sex with Sheila and if she didn't like it he would break her neck. Matters finally got to a head and Sheila walked out on him. He came down to the Mill Inn, Stonehaven, and threatened he would shoot her, the kids and me if she did not go back. She did not go back but went to stay in the Bay Hotel. She was forcibly removed at 3 a.m. approximately the following morning. She went to their family doctor who immediately phoned Max. I have missed out a bit. She went to their family doctor to complain about Maxie's strange sexual ideas and the doctor immediately phoned Max. When she got home he twisted her arm so far up her back that she had to get the doctor who was told by Max that she fell. Shortly after this incident I was walking down to the Marine Hotel from my house. I was set upon in an alley and received a slight slash on the face accompanied by the words—'That's a present from the skipper.' As I had only called Max skipper when we were flying, I assumed it was from him. I approached him the next time I saw him and he said 'You won't get the chance to run next time.' A few months after this I received a call from Sheila at about half past six, in the evening that was. She came into the house and said Max had sent her down to borrow a record of mine. She had been told not to come back to Cairnbeg until the back of nine. The following day I again received a call at about 3.45 in the afternoon and Max had sent her down to spend the rest of the afternoon and evening with me and not to back go to Cairnbeg until 8 p.m. The last time I saw Max was in the Crown Hotel one Sunday night. About six weeks later I received a call from Sheila to go down to Cairnbeg. When I arrived there I found her in a terrible state. She said he had come in and was pouring himself a drink so she went up to bed. She said that a while later he had come up the stair carrying a rifle and told her that if she didn't let him put it up her arse he would shoot her. He had stripped and got on to the bed. There had been a grab for the gun and a struggle and he got shot. This is where I come in now. I rolled him up in a sheet and a bit of canvas groundsheet, trailed [dragged] him downstairs and put him in his car then drove it. I've missed out a bit about cleaning up. I got a cloth with water and with Sheila cleaned up the mess. I then drove the car to a point near Lauriston Castle, removed the body from the back seat and pulled it through the grass. I used to stay [live] in this area and remembered an old tunnel I used to play in. I left the body in this tunnel and covered it with rocks. I drove the car to the airfield, locked it and hitch-hiked back to Aberdeen. I threw the keys of the car into the mouth of the Dee. That's it.'

In contrast, Peters's statement to the police read:

'He brought it up at work a few weeks before. He just said he was wanting to get rid of the bloke and would I come with him so that he could have transport. Well on the night I picked him up at Mr Birse's house; we went from there to Stonehaven—no we didn't, we went straight through Stonehaven out the coast road and we stopped at a little pub and had a drink in there and then we went and carried on on that road and we made for Laurencekirk. We stopped in Laurencekirk and had one drink there too. We went from there to West Cairnbeg and we parked the car on the road that runs along the back of the house. We went from there into the garage and Mrs Garvie let us into the house. Brian got the gun fae [from] the back of the door and we went through tae the sitting room. We got a drink fae Mrs Garvie and then she showed us tae the room upstairs. We waited there till Mr Garvie came home and went to bed and when he was asleep his wife came through and told us. Then we went through and Brian had the gun and he hit him on the back of the head with the butt of the gun and then he shot him with the gun, then we tied him up in a plastic groundsheet and we took him doon tae the car then Brian took his car to the airfield and I followed. We then took him to the place where we left him. I burned the groundsheet, I put some petrol on it and set fire to it. That's just more or less it.'

The statement made by Mrs Sheila Garvie read as follows:

'On Tuesday the 14th of May my husband arrived home just after eleven and we had a drink and watched television. Went to bed about 11.30 p.m. Max had two Soneryls. I fell asleep and I expect he must have been sleeping too. I wakened with someone standing and whispering to me to get up. The bedroom light was off but the room was lit from the light on the landing. I recognised the figure and the voice as being that of Brian Tevendale. He took me by the arm out to the landing and standing there was a fair-haired man. I didn't know who he was at all. I was hustled through to the bathroom and told to get in and stay there. I noticed he was carrying a gun. I didn't know at that time that it belonged to Max. I heard our bedroom door closing and terrible thumping noises. About five minutes later Brian came through and tried the handle, but I had it locked. I opened the door. He said something like 'you won't have any more of him to put up with' and asked me to stay beside the girls' door in case they came out. The two of them were a while in the bedroom and they were pulling Max out in a groundsheet type of thing. I can't remember whether they took sheets with them or not because I was terribly upset—in a helluva state—but I do remember they weren't long in going away. The following— oh now wait a minute—I was going to explain I heard one car leaving but they had already told me that this Alan had a car parked in the side road. Brian phoned on the Wednesday morning about 6 o'clock to say they had left Max's clothes in the garage and I got distressed on the phone and Brian told me to take the clothes in to Trudy (his sister's) and she would get rid of them. From that I took it that she knew of what had happened. He told me that night (on the Tuesday) that if I squealed he would get me involved and get about twenty-five years in prison. When I asked him how he was going to get away with it he said he was going to hide the body, and I asked him where and he said he wouldn't tell me. I phoned Trudy on the Wednesday night as I was in a state about the mattress which was saturated with blood. She said that she and Brian would come down and take away the mattress—I can't remember whether it was the Wednesday or the Thursday that they came down and she brought her mattress from her bed and she bought a new mattress and she said I could pay her eighteen pounds. I can't remember but I think it was the Sunday night I was in there and I was well aware that Fred Birse knew what had happened and the gun was mentioned and he advised me to wipe the gun with an oily cloth for fingerprints. Oh yes I was told by Brian that the car had got stuck and a man had pulled them out but I was never told where or by whom. I think that car has been sold now. This lad Alan, I don't know his last name, stayed [lived] with his wife in a caravan and they now stay in Fort Augustus; apparently he has got a job there. They used to visit the Birses quite often after that.'

At the beginning of my interview with Mrs Garvie I did not tell her about these statements. I merely asked her to tell me the whole story. Hesitantly at first, and then with increasing confidence, she did so.

She told me how her marriage had begun to deteriorate

after Max Garvie had become depraved in his sexual tastes and demands, and how they had quarrelled repeatedly about it.

'What were those demands?' I asked.

'I can't speak to you about it,' she told me. 'It was revolting. I don't think even prostitutes would have done what he wanted.'

She told me that she had been reduced to such a state of nervous tension and despondency that she had contemplated suicide but dismissed that solution when she thought of her children.

Now well into her story, she had lost much of her initial shyness. She was indignant when she recalled the incident of the nude photographs. 'I thought it was an unspeakable thing to do and I felt degraded. We had a row about it and Max told me that I was a prude. We had terrible arguments too about whether our two young daughters should practise nudism. I was adamant that they shouldn't.'

Despite what had happened she made references to the past which indicated just how much love there had been between them. 'It didn't happen overnight,' she said. 'He was a brilliant man and a very popular one.'

She told me of the entrance of Brian Tevendale into their lives and of the foursome that had been formed with Trudy Birse.

'I was very upset and knew what was happening was wrong,' Mrs Garvie told me 'but he just kept on saying that this was 1967 and it was the sort of 'in' thing. He still wanted me to do abnormal things even more than before. I didn't know where to turn and eventually I told my mother about it, although I was ashamed and it was a most difficult thing to do.'

I felt that she was being honest and I could understand what had happened. She had been thrown into Tevendale's arms by her husband and eventually had sought refuge in the affair with a younger and more normal man.

When Mrs Garvie had told me her version of the events of the night of the murder, I produced the statements of Tevendale and Peters. These I read over to her.

When I read Peters's story she said 'That's a lie! I wouldn't have needed to let them in: there was no lock on the garage door. The garage door was always left open, as the mechanism to open it from the cars was not working. The lock was fitted after the date of his murder.'

I now had several lines of enquiry and left Craiginches to pursue them. The first step was to interview Trudy Birse, as she would obviously be a main witness about Sheila Garvie's attitude and actions both before and after the event. Accordingly I wrote to her and arranged an interview in the Station Hotel, Aberdeen. This was followed by another meeting in the same place to go over the precognition and to make sure that my ears had not deceived me on the first occasion.

Trudy Birse was a tall, blonde, attractive woman who—as it turned out—was the reverse of reticent about her part in the affair. She seemed proud rather than ashamed of her involvement and she was eager to talk. I am a bit short of hair, but what I had almost stood on end in the course of her matter-of-fact revelations, which were delivered in the broadest of broad Aberdeen accents. She told me that she had first met Maxie in the company of her brother and Sheila and immediately felt a strong attraction for Maxie. He had told her that he liked to see Sheila and her brother enjoying themselves, and he invited her to come for a flight in his plane. She accepted the invitation enthusiastically and during the flight an assignation was made for her house in Aberdeen while her husband was absent on duty. In the house they had intercourse for the first time. Later in their enthusiasm they had a second session in his car.

She then, in astonishingly frank detail, confirmed Sheila Garvie's story of the remarkable sexual behaviour of the foursome and spoke of Garvie's strange desires and peculiar attitude towards Sheila. She confirmed that Brian and Max Garvie sometimes tossed a coin for Sheila when she, Trudy, was not present. This she had been told by Maxie. Once, when Max had lost twice in a row, he insisted that the next time all three should sleep together.

Trudy went on to relate the happenings at the strange

155

party in West Cairnbeg at which her husband and another woman were present. There had been candlelight, drinks and soft romantic music. Eventually Brian and Sheila had paired off and had gone to bed, as had Trudy and Max, leaving Trudy's husband with the other woman. (During the trial, to the accompaniment of great mirth, she was asked if the quartet had now become a sextet!) She also revealed that her husband had not been too keen to go to the party. They had had a long, detailed discussion for two days prior to it. I was not at all surprised!

She went on to say that Maxie took drugs, he drank to excess and his sexual appetites were abnormal. 'Not that I minded that,' she hastened to assure me. 'Sheila hated it, but it didn't bother me!' She and Maxie must indeed have been an acrobatic couple, for Trudy blandly revealed that on one occasion they had performed together in the cramped cockpit of Max's aircraft as it flew over the Mearns!

On the morning after the murder Brian had told Trudy that Max was dead. He said subsequently that Alan Peters had struck the farmer with an iron bar and that he, Brian, had shot him—thinking he was already dead. Later, Trudy Birse told me, Sheila had telephoned her and had come to her house. When she learned that Brian had told Trudy what had happened, Sheila said 'There was no other way, it had to be done. I couldn't take it any more.' This, of course, could be construed as incriminating Sheila, or it could be construed as her explanation for Tevendale's actions.

Trudy Birse then went on to outline the astonishing story of how she and her brother—and, incredibly enough, her policeman husband—had destroyed the blood-soaked mattress and some clothing in an attempt to cover up the crime. The general tenor of her astonishingly candid precognition was that the part Sheila Garvie played was to get rid of incriminating evidence after the event and that she, Trudy, had done all she could to help.

I had never interviewed anyone quite like Trudy Birse. She was the complete extrovert, revelling in her association with Max Garvie and their sexual exploits. During the trial she boasted 'He told me that he had told his wife that he had

had more pleasure from myself in two weeks than he had ever had from her in their married life!'

In the light of this precognition I was reasonably hopeful. What Sheila Garvie had done did not make her an accessory to murder, as in Scots Law one cannot be an accessory after the event (although the position in England is different). I did not know then that Trudy Birse would add an additional revelation when the case came to Court. Whether she deliberately concealed it from me, later concocted it, or was quite simply muddled into saying it, I shall never know.

The body of the murdered Max Garvie might never have been found, of course, had Sheila Garvie's mother, Mrs Edith Watson, not gone to the police. My next—somewhat unnerving—task, therefore, was to visit Mrs Watson, who at that time was living in the farmhouse at West Cairnbeg.

She was a kindly, motherly woman, saddened, weary and very conscious of the fact that she had in effect betrayed her daughter. She had known all along what was going on among the errant four and she and her husband did all they could to put a stop to it. Such goings-on were quite alien to her nature and she had felt completely out of her depth. Tears streamed down her cheeks as she told me 'If Sheila had given up seeing Brian after the murder, I would have taken the secret with me to my grave!'

She told me that Sheila had ignored all her entreaties to stop seeing Tevendale. She had been completely infatuated by him. In despair, Mrs Watson had decided to bring the affair to an end for the sake of the children.

Before I left there was a poignant moment when Mrs Watson showed me a letter she had received from Buckingham Palace. In desperation she had written to the Queen appealing for intervention on behalf of her daughter. The reply, from the Secretary, regretfully informed her that Her Majesty could not interfere.

While I was there, I took the opportunity to examine the farmhouse, particularly the garage and the connecting door to the house. I noticed that the latter had a Yale lock, but Mrs Watson advised me that at the date of the murder there had been no lock on that door.

The Trial

Having completed all my initial enquiries I now had to consider briefing Counsel. Since the case was one of major importance, I approached one of the ablest QCs in Scotland, Mr Lionel Daiches. To assist I obtained the help of two advocates, Mr Brian Gill and the Hon Robert Younger. Having given them a briefing on the evidence and shown them the alleged voluntary statements of the three accused, we came to the point where a decision of the utmost importance had to be taken. Should we or should we not launch an all-out attack on the character of Maxwell Garvie? This would be an attack which would blacken his memory for ever. On the one hand, we feared that members of the jury might consider it a despicable thing to do—to brand a man who could not answer as a pervert who degraded his wife by sexual malpractices. On the other, I was convinced—and, more importantly, Lionel Daiches was convinced—that it had to be done to show that Sheila Garvie had found herself in an impossible situation. This, of course, would not excuse murder, but at least it would make her behaviour understandable and her evidence credible.

Leading this kind of evidence was very much a two-edged sword but it was likely that much of it would emerge in the Crown case anyway. We decided, however, to take no risk. We had to make the decision at this time for if the defence elects to attack the character of a prosecution witness, notice must be given to the Crown in order that the allegations, if untrue or malicious, can be rebutted. Maxwell Garvie, of course, was not a witness but in fairness we felt it necessary to advise the Crown that we intended to impugn his memory. (This is a Scottish procedure which, to my mind, is eminently fair.) I was aware, of course, that indignant rebuttals would come from Max Garvie's friends, who regarded him as a fine specimen of manhood.

The next step was to introduce Sheila Garvie to Counsel. I had visited her at Craiginches about a dozen times by this time and I was now fully in her confidence, but confronted for the first time with three strangers she was again timid and mistrustful. Lionel Daiches, in his inimitable manner, helped to restore her confidence and she replied to his searching questions in a firm voice. We reassured her as best we could and left for a lengthy consultation in the Station Hotel.

Unfortunately we were completely in the dark as to the tactics to be adopted by Counsel for the other two accused— Dr R R Taylor, QC and Mr M R Kay for Peters, and Mr K G Cameron, QC and Mr J C McInnes for Tevendale. Possibly they would object to the admissibility of the alleged voluntary statements made by their clients. Peters's statement in particular was very damaging to Mrs Garvie. On paper, of course, it was not evidence against her, not having been made her presence, and the presiding judge would so direct the jury. But, as Lionel Daiches said, 'To ask a jury to ignore what they have heard is like asking them to handle a skunk and then forget about the smell!'

On 8 November, at a Pleading Diet in Stonehaven Sheriff Court, Alan Peters, Sheila Watson or Garvie and Brian Gordon Tevendale were charged that on 14 or 15 May 1968 in the farmhouse at West Cairnbeg, Fordoun, Kincardineshire they assaulted Maxwell Garvie, struck him on the head with the butt of a rifle or an iron bar or similar instrument, shot him in the head and murdered him.

A Note was lodged on behalf of Mrs Garvie giving notice that she intended to attack the character of her dead husband 'in respect of his unnatural and perverted practices'. Thus came the first hint to the general public of the sensations which were to follow.

In the light of the contradictory statements made by the other two accused, a special defence was lodged on behalf of Mrs Garvie incriminating the other accused. This, of course, was a superfluous procedure because any one of the several co-accused can accuse another, but we felt that we should make the position perfectly clear. We were alleging that the others alone had committed the crime. Peters lodged an unusual defence—that of incrimination of the other two and coercion. It was alleged that the murder had been committed by Tevendale and Mrs Garvie and that 'any acts done by Peters in connection with the murder were on the coercion of

159

Brian Tevendale'. This special defence had never been used successfully in Scotland, although as Lord Thomson, the presiding judge, was later to point out, that did not mean that it might not one day prove successful.

We had waited with interest for what would be known in cricketing terms as 'the batting order'. Crown Counsel has the privilege of selecting the order in which the accused appear on the indictment and therefore the order in which they will give evidence in Court if they so elect. We had guessed, rightly as it turned out, that Peters would want to go into the witness box in an attempt to clear himself while Tevendale would probably be held back. We hoped for an order of Tevendale/Garvie/Peters, or alternatively Garvie/Tevendale/Peters, but the astute Crown had come to the same conclusion as ourselves and charged them in the order Peters/Garvie/Tevendale knowing full well that Peters would choose to go into the box. What he had to say would then become evidence against the others.

The trial began on Tuesday 19 November 1968.

I shall not trouble the reader with too many details of the evidence. What most of the witnesses said has already been covered either in Sheila Garvie's narrative or my own. Suffice it to say that the Crown was represented by the Solicitor General, Ewan G F Stewart, MC, QC, (now Lord Stewart, one of Her Majesty's judges) and advocates, Mr Hugh D B Morton and Mr John Wheatley. They were as formidable a trio as one could find at the Scottish Bar.

The evidence from the Crown lasted six days. There was a lengthy interruption for a trial within a trial concerning the admissibility of Tevendale's statements to the police. It was alleged that these had been unfairly obtained. (This was an exact parallel to the objection Peter Manuel took in the famous trial of that revolting man.)

In the course of the trial also, the police gave evidence of the dramatic discovery of the body. Apparently when Tevendale was detained, detective constables had gone to the room where he was pacing to and fro. Suddenly Tevendale blurted out 'Get a car and I will take you to the body at Lauriston!' The officers cautioned him and advised him to get legal advice but he simply said 'Let's go. I didn't shoot him, but I will tell you about that after.'

Two cars then left Bucksburn Headquarters, taking their direction from Tevendale just as Peter Manuel had directed the police to the body of Isabelle Cooke. Tevendale directed them to drive along the Laurencekirk road then left on to the Mains of Woodstone road, told them to stop at a wooden gate and led them by torchlight through shrubbery and between trees. He stopped and said 'He is down there and along this way', indicating the direction. The time was now 5 a.m. The police could see an old cycle-frame lying partly covered by growing grass. Removal of the cycle-frame and pieces of tree roots revealed a hole in the ground leading to a shaft some nine feet deep and two feet square. By torchlight, the police crawled along the tunnel for some fifteen yards and came upon an object covered with stones. Squatting on top of one of the stones was a large toad. Some of the stones were removed, revealing a body wrapped in a sheet. The stones were replaced and photographs were taken of the body, which, with some difficulty, was eventually removed.

In those first six days of the trial there were several moments of high drama other than the account of the discovery of the body, and these moments remain etched in my memory. The press had a field day as sensation followed sensation. The listeners in the packed public galleries, apart from occasional gasps of surprise at the more titillating evidence, were held silent and spellbound.

One of the first witnesses for the Crown was the wan and pale Mrs Edith Watson, Sheila Garvie's mother. She was a tragic figure. When asked if she saw her daughter in Court she looked towards the dock and collapsed. The Court was adjourned until she appeared on the following morning. She was in tears while she told how, after his disappearance, she had asked Sheila if Max was dead. 'She nodded her head,' said Mrs Watson. 'I said "Oh, the poor beggar!" I felt so shocked and stunned. I asked her if Max had suffered and she said "No!" She mentioned having a strong man at her back. I asked her if the man was Tevendale and she just nodded her head.'

In a barely audible voice Mrs Watson recounted the agony of her decision to go to the police. The tension at this point was too much for one member of the jury, who was led ashen-faced from the court after fainting in the jury box. The trial eventually proceeded with only fourteen jurors.

There were loud gasps from the public gallery when Mrs Watson went on to confirm the Jekyll-and-Hyde nature of Max Garvie. Lionel Daiches, in cross-examination, continued the demolition of the character of the dead man.

'Trudy Birse said that she could cope with Max's sex demands where your daughter could not?'

'Yes,' came the reply.

'Did you think that he got some kind of twisted kick about imagining his wife being made love to by Brian Tevendale?'

'Yes, I think so.'

The frail old lady revealed that at one stage Garvie had admitted that he had tossed a coin with Brian Tevendale to see who would sleep with her daughter first. 'It was horrible,' she said. 'It had a terrible effect on my daughter: she was on the verge of a nervous breakdown.'

On the third day came one of the most macabre and dramatic moments I have ever experienced in a courtroom.

Prior to the trial I had examined all the Crown productions in Stonehaven Court, one of which was contained in a brown cardboard box about the size of a hat-box. The Sheriff Clerk passed it to me without any comment. I opened it and peered inside. Revealed to my startled eyes was a complete human skull: the skull of Max Garvie.

At the trial this production was tersely labelled 'No 14: skull'—a true example of economy of words! When it was shown to witnesses, the Solicitor General tactfully asked them to look into the box—but on the third day, during the testimony of a forensic expert from the University of Aberdeen, such niceties went by the board.

The doctor was describing, in great detail, the position and trajectory of the bullet which was found in Max Garvie's head. First he demonstrated to the fascinated jury on his own head. Then he was asked to look at the contents of production 14 and the box was placed on the ledge of the witness box. The good doctor was by now so immersed in his subject and the intricacies of his forensic demonstration that to my horror he put his hand into the box. I knew immediately that he was going to produce the skull and I leaned back and whispered to the stricken Mrs Garvie 'Close your eyes!' To my relief she did so.

Sublimely unaware of the impact the gruesome unveiling would have on the spectators, the doctor held the ivory skull aloft in his left hand while illustrating his points with the right. For a transient moment I imagined him saying 'Alas, poor Max, I knew him well!' Completely oblivious to the sensation he was causing, the doctor continued to lecture the jury as if they were students, unaware of the dramatic force of the hollow eye-sockets gazing mournfully out over the court. It was an electrifying moment and a grisly last appearance for Max Garvie.

These tumultuous events aside, the evidence of Trudy Birse was arguably the most sensational of the whole trial. I have covered most of it in discussing the precognitions I took from her but I mentioned then that there was something else which Trudy Birse had not said to me. It was an omission which played an absolutely vital part in the case as far as Sheila Garvie was concerned.

When I had spoken to Trudy she told me, not once but two or three times, that Brian had told her that he and Peters had been responsible for the murder. There had been no mention of Sheila Garvie being involved before the killing.

In the witness box she repeated the same story almost verbatim but now, in subtle examination in chief, there were some sensational additions. There was a series of rapid questions from the Solicitor General and in the midst of these Trudy burst into tears. Her answers emerged as nails in Sheila Garvie's legal coffin and I am convinced today that her replies were an unexpected bonus to the Solicior General. She now said that Brian had told her that Sheila had let them in at West Cairnbeg, had hidden them in an empty bedroom and had come and told them when Max Garvie was asleep. She then added, and this was the killer, that Sheila Garvie was there when Brian said it. I could hardly believe that I had heard this. I leaned over and whispered to Lionel Daiches 'She certainly never said anything of that nature to me!'

I glanced at Mrs Garvie. Her face was set and very pale. With Peters's probable testimony to add to this, we now had two people giving evidence that she had been involved in the murder before it was committed.

Needless to say Lionel Daiches cross-examined Trudy Birse very closely and emphatically. At one stage, flustered and near to tears, she said to him 'I don't really know what happened!' Then she broke down. When she recovered she nonetheless continued to maintain that Mrs Garvie had let Tevendale and Peters into the farmhouse and later told them Max Garvie was asleep. This information had been given to her by her brother in the presence of Sheila Garvie. Mr Daiches continued to press and she broke down again and sobbed 'I think it was the most dreadful thing that could happen to anyone!' Then, after a lull to allow her to recover, she added 'It is very difficult for me to speak calmly about what happened to him.'

Difficult or not, irreparable damage had been done to Sheila Garvie's defence. Why Trudy Birse made the damaging addition to her story I will never know. It has always remained a mystery to me, but I will discuss my own theory later. When Court was adjourned I hurried immediately to see Mrs Garvie. She was as staggered as I had been by Trudy Birse's statements. 'How could she say something like that?' she kept repeating. 'How could she do it to me?' Stunned as she was, the full import of what had happened had not yet become apparent, however, and I felt this was not the time to labour the point.

The Crown case eventually closed. The defence of Alan Peters was first, and naturally he went into the witness box. He told of his first meeting with Tevendale and the friendship which developed. He said he had not realised what was going to happen when they visited West Cairnbeg together on the night of 14 May and were led from the garage into the house by Mrs Garvie. Thereafter he went along with what Tevendale did, in fear that, if he refused, he would get the same. He said that Mrs Garvie had left them in a darkened bedroom for about half an hour before coming back to tell them that Max Garvie was asleep. Tension mounted in court as he recounted 'We came out of the room and Brian Tevendale said "Follow me." We went across the landing and into another bedroom. In that room there was a man lying asleep on the bed. Brian went up to the right-hand side of the bed and told me to stay back. He struck the man several times on the back of the head, then picked up a pillow, threw it on his head and shot him through the pillow once.'

This remarkable story was of course a reiteration of his statement to the police but it now was evidence and, along with Trudy Birse's amended recollections, it was most damaging to Sheila Garvie.

Peters was rigorously cross-examined by Lionel Daiches but he stuck to what he said.

He was supported in his defence by his wife. It was very clever court-craft on the part of Dr Taylor to lead this pathetic girl, as she was far advanced in pregnancy and would merit considerable sympathy from the jurors. By such things are they moved. Her main theme was that her husband was scared stiff of violence and would have done whatever he was told to do. Good sound stuff. His sister gave similar evidence and his former headmaster deponed that Peters was cheerful, well-liked and absolutely straightforward. I had to hand it to Dr Taylor. The defence of the first accused was closed.

It was now the turn of Sheila Garvie. It was the moment all Scotland, especially those with a more prurient streak in their natures, had been waiting for. Over two hundred people who had been queuing since dawn outside the court were turned away that day.

In all, her evidence spanned three days. Throughout these days she presented a brave front but it was easy to see that the strain had told. The skin over her high cheekbones was tightly drawn and seemed to become more transparent by the hour. Her face was thinner, almost to the point of emaciation. She was weary. She was dressed as she had been throughout the trial in a powder-blue suit.

The start of the examination in chief was pure Daiches.

'Mrs Garvie, to take the oath you raised your right hand. Will you now raise your left hand?' The bemused Sheila Garvie slowly raised her left hand, and as she did her wedding ring could be seen glinting in the court lights.

'Have you ever had that ring off since the day you were married?'

'No,' came the clear reply.

She was then taken through the whole sorry story, the skeleton of which was in her voluntary statement to the police. She described in detail the change in her once-loving husband, her disgust at his malpractices. She deponed frankly about the adulterous circus and her loss of love for her husband. As she described how her husband's shrouded body was bumped down the stairs, her knuckles shone white as she gripped like a vice the rail of the witness box. She denied that she let the men into the house. She denied that she had told Trudy Birse that she had done so. She admitted her attempts to cover up the murder, but as she swayed and seemed on the point of collapse in the witness box, her most astonishing admission was 'I felt morally responsible for what had been done because I had allowed Brian to fall in love with me and had become emotionally involved with him. I felt I had unconsciously provoked him in the emotional state in which he was. I was at a crossroads in my life. I took a decision that night that whatever happened I would protect Brian.'

Towards the end of his examination Lionel Daiches turned to a subject which could well have a very adverse effect on the jury: the fact that Sheila Garvie had continued her physical relationship with Tevendale even after the murder of her husband. In reply to his questions she replied 'I was—and still am—in love with Brian.' A stir ran through the court. Mr Daiches went on.

'It may be suggested to you that, knowing what you did know of the morning of 15 May, your continued association with Brian Tevendale could only indicate a brutal indifference to your husband's murder. If that suggestion were put to you by anyone, what would you reply?'

'I would put it this way: that Brian must have done it to protect me and I felt I could not betray him.'

166

The last question came. 'And lastly, Mrs Garvie, do you say now on oath that you were innocent of any complicity in your husband's murder?'

In the still courtroom came the quiet reply. 'I am.'

Dr Taylor, for Peters, followed by the Solicitor General, then put her through one of the longest and most gruelling cross-examinations I have ever heard. Throughout the extended agony of this relentless probing, filled with suggestions pointing to guilty knowledge, she steadfastly refused to depart from the accounts she had given to the police. Eventually, after a period of time which must have seemed more like three years than three days, she was allowed to regain the shelter of the dock in a state of physical and mental exhaustion.

The only other witness for the defence of Sheila Garvie was a joiner from Laurencekirk. This evidence was of great importance in the light of Peters's statement to the police that Mrs Garvie had let them in. This might well imply that without the assistance of Mrs Garvie they could not have obtained entry. This had been contradicted by Mrs Watson, who had said that in May 1968 the garage door was left open because the magic eye in the cars did not work, and that anyone who knew the house could walk in through the garage and into the washhouse and kitchen. She emphasised in the examination that the communicating door had no lock. The important evidence of the joiner was to the effect that on 12 July he fitted a lock to the connecting door and he identified the lock in a photograph which was one of the productions. He emphasised that there was no lock on that door before he fitted the Yale.

No sooner had the evidence of the joiner been completed than Mr Cameron was on his feet to announce that he would not be leading evidence. Tevendale was not going into the box!

Mr Ewan Stewart then addressed the jury, dealing in merciless detail with the incriminating evidence against all the accused. He warned that they must not be influenced by prejudice or emotion or (here a sly dig) powerful oratory.

His most telling submission was 'We know that up to the time of his death Maxwell Garvie enjoyed a good reputation locally, but we cannot shut our eyes to the evidence. He must to some extent have been a degenerate man. If he was as bad as he was made out to be, it might be that some sympathy for Sheila Garvie may emerge from that. On the other hand, it is double-edged because it may show you that she would have had a very strong motive to seek his destruction.'

Dr Taylor—for Peters—like a forensic Pontius Pilate washed his hands of the involvement of his client in the tortuous sex-life of Tevendale and Mrs Garvie. He emphasised that Peters had been deluded into the affair and had been afraid to interfere. He pointed out 'If Brian Tevendale had screwed himself up to the point where he was prepared to murder Maxwell Garvie, he would have been prepared to murder my client.' As he shrewdly put it, Peters was 'a fly drawn into the spider's web'. Dr Taylor concluded his speech knowing that he had built up a very substantial house without any straw.

It was now the turn of Lionel Daiches of the silver tongue. I have heard him address juries in hundreds of cases and have always been entranced by his powers of oratory, his command of language, his precision of speech. On this occasion he surpassed himself. He was superb. He ridiculed the depiction of Sheila Garvie as a latter day Lady Macbeth allowing the killer in to murder her husband while he was asleep. He poured scorn on the various activities of 'Turbulent Trudy' and her policeman husband. He deplored the malicious tittle-tattle which would follow Sheila Garvie to the end of her days. He ended his brilliant address to the jury by quoting John Donne in ringing tones. 'I do not seek your pity,' he concluded; 'I ask only for a verdict in accordance with justice. I do not ask you, I *demand* that you return the verdict of Not Guilty.'

When he sat down I am convinced that had the jury had the opportunity to consider their verdict that day they would have acquitted Sheila Garvie—but, alas, it was a Friday and the weekend had to pass before Lord Thomson charged the jury.

Kenneth Cameron, for Tevendale, briefly addressed the jury knowing that he had no chance, but skilfully drew attention to inconsistencies in the evidence, emphasising that the Crown was relying on Trudy Birse, Alan Peters and Sheila Garvie—all witnesses of doubtful worth.

On Monday, to a fanfare of trumpets, Lord Thomson took his seat and turned to face the expectant jurors. He was careful to point out that the court was a court of law, not of morals. It was not the function of the jury to decide whether the people concerned were moral, immoral or amoral. In a fair, lucid and comprehensive summing-up he particularly mentioned that in Peters's voluntary statement to the police there was no mention of coercion, fear or terror.

Dealing with Sheila Garvie—who, in the course of the case, had been referred to variously as Lady Macbeth, Lady Bountiful and Lady Chatterley—he advised the jury to give full regard to the whole background of events in which the killing of Max Garvie was set, and to ask themselves 'Do you believe her version of the events as given to the police and confirmed by her in the witness box, or do you believe Peters's version? . . . In practical sense your critical choice lies between Peters's account of the night of 14–15 May and Sheila Garvie's.'

He mentioned doubts regarding the evidence of Trudy Birse. 'There is in the evidence a good deal of doubt as to how much Mrs Garvie said to Mrs Birse after the murder and how much Tevendale said to Mrs Birse and how much was said when both Sheila Garvie and Tevendale were present. If you accept Mrs Birse's evidence there is evidence that Mrs Garvie said to Mrs Birse something to the effect that she had gone into the room upstairs and told Tevendale and Peters that Max was asleep. If that is true, it is a damning piece of evidence against her.'

At the end of his charge Lord Thomson was to emphasise once more that the jury would have to give some very careful consideration as to the view it was to take of the reliability of Mrs Birse's evidence.

The court adjourned. The trapdoor in the floor was opened and the three accused disappeared into the cells. The pressmen rushed out to commandeer the phones. Trudy Birse, who had been sitting at the back of the court with her husband, was loudly booed from the public gallery when she rose to speak to her mother, who was also in the court.

At five minutes to twelve there was a flurry of excitement. The jurors were returning after an absence of over an hour. The court was packed, some people standing where there were no seats. The jury filed in. The accused took their places in the dock and Lord Thomson appeared. When all was still the Clerk of the Court rose to his feet, faced the jury and said 'Who speaks for you?' The foreman of the jury, a youngish, stockily-built man, stood up.

'What is your verdict in the case of Alan Peters?'

'Not Proven.'

These two words exploded in the still of the court. For a split second there was absolute quiet followed by gasps of disbelief. Through the hubbub the foreman added that this verdict was by a majority. I knew immediately that all was lost: like those who preferred Barabbas the jury had preferred Peters. Sheila Garvie had no chance.

'What is your verdict in the case of Sheila Garvie?' intoned the Clerk.

Back came the fatal word. 'Guilty.'

'Is your verdict unanimous or by a majority?'

'By a majority.'

Tevendale was also found Guilty. This time unanimously.

There were murmurs of conversation as the Clerk recorded the verdicts. I glanced at Sheila. Her face seemed drained of blood, a deathly mask devoid of any expression.

Lord Thomson told Peters that he was free to go. The bar of the dock was raised and, looking bewildered as well he might, he slipped away to obscurity. Tevendale and Sheila Garvie were sentenced to life imprisonment. The trapdoor was opened for the last time and the lovers made their way down to the cells. I followed at once to tell her that we would consider an appeal. She was dazed and uncomprehending. She didn't seem to hear me.

In the end we decided that there were no grounds for an appeal and I had the unenviable task of telling her that there was no hope. She accepted it stoically. I think her overriding emotion at the time was simply a vast relief that the whole sorry business was over.

In closing I should add that I did not lose contact with Sheila Garvie for quite some time. During subsequent interviews concerning business matters, three things occupied her mind to the exclusion of all others.

The first and paramount one was the well-being of her children. I knew that the trustee of the estate of Max Garvie was a highly respected solicitor in Montrose. I was able to reassure her that he had the welfare of the children very much in mind. I also assured her that the children would be able to visit her from time to time.

The second matter which constantly plagued her was the evidence of Trudy Birse. When I had taken my precognition from Trudy, Sheila Garvie and I had gone over it with extreme care. At the time she had agreed that what Trudy said was substantially the truth. She could not understand why Trudy had departed from her original account. As I have already said, I was puzzled too. Trudy appeared to me to be a most unusual woman, a complete extrovert, and I was convinced then (and I am still convinced) that the version she gave me was accurate—and, more importantly, complete. She was not a malicious woman and I do not think that she deliberately lied in the witness box. When she made her damaging statement she was in tears and in a state of near hysteria. Clever and encouraging examination in chief could have led to the damning declaration. Later under cross-examination by Lionel Daiches she again broke down at the vital moment. Mr Daiches suggested that her emotional feelings had become involved and her recollections had become dimmed. I tend to agree with him. In my opinion she really did not know what she was saying.

It could be argued, of course, that vengeance might have played a part since she thought that Sheila had been privy to the murder of the man she loved. Somehow I do not believe this to be true. Public hostility towards her, both during the trial and after the trial, did not upset her in the least. She was the greatest enigma in the case.

The third matter on Sheila's mind was Tevendale. She

171

had vowed her undying love for him in the court and yet he had not given evidence which might have seen her step from the dock a free woman. Obviously Tevendale had been properly advised by Counsel not to leave the security of the dock for the hazards of the witness box. Nonetheless, his silence was hardly the action of an erstwhile lover, since he must have realised that he himself was doomed. Tevendale's silence had obviously shaken Sheila but it was only later—when I informed her that I had been told that Tevendale was negotiating with a Sunday newspaper for the sale of loveletters she had sent to him—that her devotion to him was killed. During subsequent visits to see her at Gateside, she never referred to him again. She did, however, frequently refer to Trudy Birse.

During the trial it had been suggested that she might have had a monetary motive for wanting to get rid of Max Garvie. He was, after all, a wealthy man. When I brought up the question of his estate she was quite adamant that she wanted nothing whatever to do with the estate and she instructed me so to advise the trustee.

Some time later I was approached by a film producer who wanted to film the story, starring Maggie Smith as Sheila Garvie. I told Sheila this but she would have nothing whatever to do with it, despite the fact that a very substantial sum of money was mentioned.

Over the years I noticed interesting changes in Mrs Garvie. At first she was despondent and desperate to see her children. I feared that she would vegetate but, happily, these fears were not realised. She grew thinner but the handsome bone-structure of her face would never change. Her hair, which had been tinted blonde, reverted to its natural brown colour. She wore it severely and neatly styled, not now by an expensive stylist but by her own hands. She was always neatly dressed in the not unattractive prison frocks. As time went on she responded to the help and counsel of the Governor, Lady Martha Bruce, a lady of remarkable vision in the field of penal reform. Eventually Sheila emerged from her cocoon of despair, not as a useless butterfly but as one who pollinated others with useful advice, help and information. She conducted a series of lectures in prison on subjects such as cookery, hairstyling, good housekeeping and the use of cosmetics. Thus not only did she prepare other prisoners for freedom, she prepared herself. The striking features of a remarkable case which linger in my mind are Sheila Garvie's hopeless infatuation with Tevendale—her prejudicial and unrepentant association with him after the murder—the betrayal by her distraught mother—the egregious Trudy Birse—the anomaly of the three diametrically opposed and totally irreconcilable voluntary statements—the probing cross-examination of Ewan Stewart—the speech by Lionel Daiches—the remarkable forensic triumph of Dr Taylor—and last, but above all, the yellowed skull of Maxwell Garvie gazing out over the courtroom.

Was Sheila Garvie guilty? I for one did not doubt her story, nor apparently did a minority of the jury. As Paul Harris so succinctly puts it in his account of the trial: 'Did the Crown prove she was guilty beyond reasonable doubt? If a minority of the jury are not in favour of a guilty verdict, surely reasonable doubt must exist.' To my mind the story told to the police by Peters that Mrs Garvie let them in, thus implying that they could not gain entry without her, was completely refuted by the evidence of her mother and the joiner about the fitting of the Yale lock. In examination in chief Peters did not say that Mrs Garvie let them in but said that she met them at the end of a corridor. Skilful examination in chief caused him to alter that to the beginning of a corridor.

I still wonder where the truth lies.